NATIONAL FORECLOSURE CATALOG

Nationwide Access to Foreclosed Real Estate

This publication is designed to provide accurate and authoritative information. It is sold with the understanding that the publisher is not engaged in rendering legal, accounting, or other professional services. If legal or other expert assistance is required, the services of an individual who is a competent professional should be sought.

TENTH EDITION

ISBN 0-9647365-1-9

Published and sold by Bargain Property Network

Printed in the United States of America.

Foreword

Congratulations! You now have in your hands the nation's premier guide to bargain home-buying. The *National Foreclosure Catalog* gives you all the information you need to find great deals on real estate and government foreclosures. And once you've found the foreclosure bargain that's right for you, the *National Foreclosure Catalog* shows you how to obtain affordable financing—even if you have less than perfect credit and very little money for a down payment.

In addition to this valuable information, you're now enrolled as a member of our National Foreclosure Program, with ongoing access to current foreclosed property listings in your area. This program has two parts:

• **Foreclosed Property Listings.** This list of foreclosed properties has been prepared just for you from our nationwide database of over 30,000 foreclosed properties. You'll find page after page of foreclosures in your area. These listings are updated every two weeks, and upon request, these updated lists will be sent to you free of charge. That way you'll always have a wide selection of opportunities at your fingertips! Updated listings are available to our members, by mail, just call our Customer Service Department at (800) 333-1915 and request your update. Or log on to our website at: **www.bargainproperty.com** and follow the online instructions to obtain your updates.

• **This catalog.** The *National Foreclosure Catalog* tells you HOW to use the listings. You'll learn the secrets of identifying the property that's right for you, how to work with a real estate agent or broker, and how to get a loan. In other words, this catalog supplies the basic tools you need to make your dream of home ownership a reality! Plus, because new properties are always coming on the market, this catalog includes Appendices that give you the addresses, phone numbers and web addresses of local government agency offices. You'll be able to do what the real pros do and call these offices yourself. That way you will learn about the best deals that much sooner and improve your chances of success!

This information is now yours to use in your search for foreclosed real estate. Happy bargain hunting!

—Bargain Property Network

Online Translation Available:

If you speak one of these five languages–Spanish, French, Italian, German or Portuguese–simply log on to our website:

www.bargainproperty.com

Click on "**FOR LIVE HELP**" and you'll be helped to translate our web pages into your own language.

Table of Contents

1 How To Get Started Now

Maybe you always thought home ownership was a dream beyond your reach. Think again! With the Foreclosed Property Listings we have provided and the National Foreclosure Catalog, you're ready to take advantage of some of the nation's best deals on foreclosed real estate.

This two-part program is especially designed to make it easy for you to find affordable housing in your area. If you haven't already done so, turn to the customized Foreclosed Property Listings that accompany this catalog and take a look at the substantial number of listings in your part of the country.

Where Do These Listings Come From?

Your Foreclosed Property Listings are compiled from the latest available property lists put out by private lenders, government agencies, and government-sponsored institutions, including:

- Banks, insurance companies, and other private mortgage lenders
- Fannie Mae (Federal National Mortgage Association, or FNMA)
- Freddie Mac (Federal Home Loan Mortgage Corporation, or FHLMC)
- Small Business Administration (SBA)
- Federal Deposit Insurance Corporation (FDIC)
- Farmer's Home Administration (FmHA; recently renamed RECDS, or Rural Economic and Community Development Services)

As you can see, there are so many listings that you may wonder, "How will I ever be able to call them all?" The answer is, "you don't." Just call ONLY the ones that are of the greatest interest to you! Here's a strategy you can use to get the maximum benefit from these listings and find the home you want FAST!

BUYER'S TIP:
Keep in mind that government agencies are not always quick to remove listings that have sold. The status of listings and brokers changes from time to time. So don't be discouraged if someone else has snapped up a property you called on—just keep calling, and you're sure to succeed!

Scan the Listings

The best way to sort through your Foreclosed Property Listings is by address. Scan the listings and circle or use a highlighter pen to mark the properties located in neighborhoods where you would want to live.

You may want to scan the listings more than once. It's easy to miss something the first time through. You also may want to do half the listings now and the other half later, especially if you come up with many possibilities that interest you!

Once you've gotten your addresses all marked, it's time to use the rest of the information included with the listings to narrow your choices down even further. Now we'll take you step by step through the rest of the items so you know what each one means.

How To Read the Listings

1. Sale Type. On almost every listing, this says REO. REO means Real Estate Owned. It is another term for a real estate foreclosure that has been taken over by a private lender or a government agency.

2. Property Type. This tells you what kind of property is for sale. Some of the types you'll find in your Foreclosed Property Listings are: Residential Unit, House, Single Family Lot, Condo, Multifamily, Commercial, Industrial, and Other.

3. Location. This tells you the locations of the properties. It gives you the street address, town, and zip code. Use this information to help find a home in the location you want to live in.

4. Listing Agency and Contact. These lines tell you what agency and/or individual is in charge of selling the property. Opposite their names are the phone numbers to call for details.

BUYER'S TIP

You will see the term REO used throughout the Foreclosed Property Listings and this catalog. REO means Real Estate Owned, and it's just another term for a foreclosed property that's been taken over by a private lender or government agency.

What To Do When You Call

Now that you know exactly what properties you want to learn more about, it's time to call the contact numbers and do just that. Start out by giving the address and ID number of the property and ask if it's still available. If so, you can then ask to see the property.

The agent in charge of the sale will come out, show you the property, and explain all the terms and conditions for that property in detail. If you like what you see and want to place a bid, the agent will help you do so.

BUYER'S TIP:
If you don't find what you're looking for right away, don't worry! You can receive FREE monthly updates of your Foreclosed Property Listings by simply calling our Customer Support Department at 1-800-333-1915. As a valued member of our insider's network, call our customer support representatives with any questions or problems you may have.

About This Catalog

After you've referred to the Foreclosed Property Listings to identify properties that appeal to you, use this *National Foreclosure Catalog* for tips on inspecting the properties, working with an agent or broker, and obtaining affordable financing. You'll learn the advantages of home ownership and why foreclosures are your best bet for real estate bargains.

You'll also find detailed information on each of the government agencies and government-sponsored institutions that sell these properties. Chapters 6 through 11 and the Appendices are packed with hotline phone numbers you can use to call the agencies directly. It's important for you to supplement the Foreclosed Property Listings we've provided with the late-breaking information you can only get by calling the agencies directly.

It's not necessary to read this entire catalog at once. Just get an overview first, then come back later to the parts that interest you the most. If you need help reading the Foreclosed Property Listings that accompany this catalog, turn to Chapter 1 for assistance. You might then want to turn to the chapters on the agencies selling the specific properties you selected from the Foreclosed Property Listings.

Next you might read Chapter 2, which reviews the many advantages of home ownership and explains why foreclosures are your best bet for real estate bargains. Chapter 3 contains a guide to finding the home you really want, including a home inspection checklist. Then you can read about real estate brokers (Chapter 4) and how to get a loan (Chapter 5).

If you run into any unfamiliar terms, consult the Glossary in the back of the catalog. And in the Appendices, you'll find addresses and phone numbers of agency offices near you that provide you with information on even more real estate bargains!

Taken together, we think you'll agree that your Foreclosed Property Listings and the *National Foreclosure Catalog* form a one, two punch that will put you in the winner's circle! So now, it's time to get started. We wish you very happy hunting!

2 The Benefits of Home Ownership

Have you been wondering whether you'd REALLY be better off buying a home instead of renting? If so, you share a common concern. While it does take an investment of time to find the right home, and a certain investment of money to buy that home, we're willing to bet that the time and money you spend will be well worth it—and probably far less than you might think!

This chapter explains the benefits of home ownership and gives you a list of questions to ask yourself when you're getting ready to buy. You'll also find two handy charts on pages 16 and 17 that show you at a glance how much your monthly payment will be, plus a summary of the major steps in buying a home for future reference.

So Why Buy?

There are five main reasons to start enjoying the rewards of home ownership today:

• **Home ownership means big tax advantages.** You can deduct the entire amount of your mortgage interest from Federal income taxes—and in most states, you can deduct this amount from your state taxes, too. When you realize that interest makes up nearly all your monthly payment for half the term of your mortgage, that adds up to huge savings year after year! You're also allowed to deduct what you pay in property taxes on your income tax return. That's a far cry from the renting scene—where what you pay every month is gone forever.

• **A home is a sound investment.** When you choose a home you can afford, the potential payoff is great. Every month when you make your mortgage payment, you're building equity in a place of your own. The longer you stay put, the more equity you have. And while there's no guarantee that your home will increase in value, many homes ARE worth far more as time goes on, which means you build even more equity. If and when you finally decide to sell, you can make a substantial profit on your investment!

• **A first home leads to a better second home.** Once you're in the housing market, it's a lot easier to move up. That means even if the home you REALLY want is beyond your financial reach at the moment, you can take a step in the right direction by buying a less expensive home today. After you hold onto the first home for a while and build up some equity, you can often sell at a profit and move up!

• **You can plan your housing costs better when you buy than when you rent.** If you've ever gotten a huge rent increase from your landlord, or been kicked out of the place you're renting with just 30 days' notice, you know exactly what we mean. Rent increases are unpredictable and normally beyond your control—and you never know when the landlord may pull out the rug from under you. But when you buy, you know exactly what your payment will be every month. Plus, there's no landlord coming by to tell you to start packing.

• **You gain the satisfaction and security of home ownership.** What does that mean? For one thing, you're free to decorate as you choose and make whatever improvements you want to your home. You'll find out first hand what "pride of ownership" really means. It's a great feeling—there's nothing else like it! Chances are you'll also put down roots and feel more a part of your community than ever before.

Questions to Ask Before You Buy

There's no right answer when it comes to buying a home. But here are some questions to help guide you in making the decision to buy.

- Do I want to stay in the area where I'm currently living? For how long?
- Do I expect to move to another town in the near future?
- Do I expect my income to change in the future? Will it go up, down, or remain the same?
- Are there other large purchases (e.g., boat, car) that are important to me?

How Much Home Can You Afford?

We have two charts to help you get an idea of how much home you can afford. Chart A on page 16 shows the results of a very simple housing formula used by the FHA (Federal Housing Administration). According to the FHA, most people can afford to put 29% of their gross monthly income toward housing costs. People with very little debt can afford even more—up to 41%! Chart A shows your annual and monthly gross income, and 29% of that amount.

Then use Chart B on page 17 to see about how much your monthly mortgage will be, based on your interest rate and how much the home you want is selling for. Please note that the figures on this chart are for monthly principal and interest payments only; your mortgage payment will also include taxes and insurance, which vary from place to place. So keep in mind that you must look for a total monthly mortgage payment that is a little less than the amounts on the chart, to allow for the taxes and insurance you'll owe every month.

BUYER'S TIP:
Shop around for the lowest interest rates in your area. As you can see from Chart B, you'll be able to afford a more expensive home if your interest rate is 7% than if it's 9%.

Chart A: 29% Of Gross Income

Annual Gross Income	Monthly Gross Income	29% of Gross Income
$15,000	$1,250	$363
$20,000	$1,667	$483
$25,000	$2,083	$604
$30,000	$2,500	$725
$35,000	$2,917	$846
$40,000	$3,333	$967
$45,000	$3,750	$1,088
$50,000	$4,167	$1,208

Chart B: Mortgage Payment Calculator

Monthly Principal and interest payments for 30-year, fixed rate mortgage. Monthly taxes and insurance are not included.

Cost	6%	6.5%	7%	7.5%	8%	8.5%	9%	9.5%	10%
$25,000	$ 150	158	166	175	183	192	201	210	219
$30,000	$ 180	190	200	210	220	231	241	252	263
$40,000	$ 240	253	266	280	293	308	322	336	351
$50,000	$ 300	316	333	350	367	384	402	420	439
$60,000	$ 360	379	399	420	440	461	483	505	527
$70,000	$ 420	442	466	489	514	538	563	589	614
$80,000	$ 480	506	532	559	587	615	644	673	702
$90,000	$ 540	569	599	629	660	692	724	757	790
$100,000	$ 600	632	665	699	734	769	805	841	878
$110,000	$ 660	695	732	769	807	846	885	925	965
$120,000	$ 719	758	798	839	880	923	966	1,009	1,053
$130,000	$ 780	822	865	909	954	1,000	1,046	1,093	1,141
$140,000	$ 839	885	931	979	1,027	1,076	1,126	1,177	1,229
$150,000	$ 899	948	998	1,049	1,101	1,153	1,207	1,261	1,316
$160,000	$ 959	1,011	1,064	1,119	1,174	1,230	1,287	1,345	1,404
$170,000	$ 1,019	1,075	1,131	1,189	1,247	1,307	1,368	1,429	1,492

Foreclosures: The Fast Track

You probably got this catalog because you know that foreclosures mean deals—and you're absolutely right! Foreclosures happen when homeowners find themselves unable to make their monthly payments. As the saying goes, their loss is your gain!

When they get far enough behind, the lender forecloses on the property, which means it is repossessed and "taken back" by the lender. The lender assumes ownership of the property and is then free to sell it to someone else—someone like you!—at a greatly reduced price.

Once the property is taken back by the lender, it is referred to as an REO. This term stands for Real Estate Owned, and it's a term you'll find throughout this catalog and your Foreclosed Property Listings as we talk about the great deals you'll find on these properties!

The 10 Steps To Home Ownership

The 10 major steps in buying a home are summarized on the next page. Use them for a handy reference as you learn about the homebuying process. The exact order of these steps may vary depending on your individual situation, but the list will help you keep everything on track.

Now it's time to turn to Chapter 3, Find The House You Really Want, and start looking!

10 Steps to Home Ownership

1. Decide how much home you can afford. (See the charts in Chapter 2)

2. Decide what kind of home you really want and need. (See Chapter 3)

3. Use the Foreclosed Property Listings and the telephone hotlines in this catalog to find the homes you like. (See Chapters 6—11)

4. Find a real estate agent or broker you like. (See Chapter 4)

5. Review the loan programs in this catalog—including special loans for people who wouldn't ordinarily qualify—and begin the process of obtaining the loan that's right for you. (See Chapter 5)

6. Fill out the Home Inspection Checklist for the homes you like. (See Chapter 3)

7. Make an offer. (See Chapter 4)

8. Apply for a mortgage loan. (See Chapter 5)

9. Close the loan. (See Chapter 5)

10. Move in and enjoy the benefits and satisfaction of home ownership.

3 Find The House You Really Want

With so many homes to choose from, how do you zero in on the one that's best for you? That's what this chapter is all about.

We'll give you a few handy guidelines to help you sort through the hundreds of bargain properties available and come up with the ones most suited to your needs.

Also, on page 25, you'll find a Home Inspection Checklist that you can use to compare the homes you've seen and remember what you like and don't like about each one.

Your Personal Shopping Lists

Even before you go out shopping for homes, it's a great idea to make two lists of your very own: your "Want List," which has all the extras you dream about having (pool, den, fireplace, rosebushes, etc.); and your "Must Have" list, which includes all the basics (how many bedrooms and baths, garage or carport, workshop, etc.).

Then, when you're trying to decide whether to visit a home or not, you can eliminate the ones that don't meet the criteria on your "Must Have" list right away. And the homes that have some extras on your "Want List" can be easily identified as hot prospects for you!

Choose Your Neighborhood Carefully

Much of your happiness in your new home will depend on the neighborhood you pick, so put some thought into your future surroundings. Do you have a young, grow-

BUYER'S TIP:
Don't forget that you have two sources of foreclosed properties at your fingertips: the Foreclosed Property Listings that were sent to you with the *National Foreclosure Catalog*; and Chapters 6 through 11 and the Appendices of this catalog, which are packed with hotline phone numbers you can use to call the agencies directly. Use these phone lines to get late-breaking listings that are only available by calling the agencies directly.

ing family? Are you retired or soon to retire? Are you married or single?

Every type of person feels at home in a different kind of neighborhood. If you have kids, you probably want a street where they will have plenty of playmates. If you're retired, you might prefer peace and quiet. If you work, you probably want a place that's not too far away from your job. If you're single, you might choose to be close to downtown and the nightlife.

To really check out the neighborhood, talk to the people who live there. Visit the neighborhood at different times of day and drive into the area from different directions. It's a good sign if the houses and yards are clean and neat. On the other hand, if commercial businesses are moving into the area, that's not such a good sign.

Just remember, the best surprise after you move in is no surprise. Don't skimp on checking out the neighborhood before you sign on the dotted line.

Diamonds in the Rough

It's important not to reject a house that has many of the things you want just because of its external appearance. With a little "sweat equity," you can easily slap on a coat of paint inside and out, and make some minor repairs.

In fact, it's a rule of thumb that one of the best houses you can buy is a fixer-upper in a good neighborhood. As long as the neighborhood is decent, the house will be worth much more than you paid for it once you've fixed it up. Then, when you resell, the phrase "diamond in the rough" will have a whole new meaning for you!

Look For Nearby Amenities

In addition to the neighborhood itself, take a look at the general area surrounding the house you want. If any of the following amenities are nearby, they may have a positive effect on the resale value of the house:

- Grocery Stores
- Parks
- Activity Centers
- Theaters
- Easy Freeway Access
- Recreational Facilities
- Restaurants
- Shopping Centers
- Places of Worship

BUYER'S TIP:
The most popular home in America is still the single family detached house. Why? It provides the most privacy, the most living space for the dollar, and the fastest increase in value over time.

Fair Housing Rights

As you start to look around at houses to buy, you'll be glad to know that you are protected by the Fair Housing Act (Title VIII of the Civil Rights Act, 1988). This law prohibits discrimination in housing because of race, color, national origin, religion, sex, handicap, or family status (i.e. whether or not you have children).

The Fair Housing Act covers most housing. Sometimes the Act does not apply to owner-occupied buildings with less than four units, single-family housing sold or rented without a broker, or housing operated by organizations and private clubs that limit occupancy to members. But in most other circumstances, the Fair Housing Act is there for you.

In practical terms, the Fair Housing Act means that a person selling a house cannot do any of the following based on race, color, national origin, religion, sex, handicap, or family status:

- Refuse to sell or negotiate for housing
- Refuse to make housing available
- Set different terms, conditions or privileges for the sale of housing

- Provide different housing services or facilities
- Falsely deny that housing is available for inspection or sale

BUYER'S TIP:
When you're shopping for homes, bring a camera with you and take plenty of pictures, both inside and out. That way, even weeks later, there won't be any doubt in your mind about what you saw!

You have the same rights when you go to apply for a mortgage. If you think your rights have been violated, you can get help from the HUD housing office nearest you. See Appendix A for a complete list of HUD offices nationwide.

Home Inspection Checklist

Use the Home Inspection Checklist on the next page to rate each home you're interested in. Bargain Property Network invites you to make copies of this page and fill out a new one for each home you visit. That way it'll be a quick and easy job to compare them and identify the home that's best for you!

Home Inspection Checklist

Home Features	Good	Average	Poor
INTERIOR			
Square footage			
Number of bedrooms			
Number of baths			
Floorplan			
Closets/storage space			
Fireplace			
Cable TV			
Living Room			
Dining Room			
Kitchen			
Appliances			
Fixtures			
Laundry Room			
Walls			
Ceilings			
Floors			
Carpets			
Stairs			
Basement			
Attic			
Garage			
Bonus Space			
Plumbing			
Electrical			
Insulation			
Heating			
Air Conditioning			
Ventilation			
Overall Interior			
EXTERIOR			
Landscaping			
Lawn/garden			
Foundation grading/draining			
Driveway			
Sidewalk			
Paint			
Windows			
Screens/storm windows			
Siding			
Doors			

Home Features	Good	Average	Poor
Porches			
Patio/Deck			
Roof			
Gutters/downspouts			
Back Yard			
Front Yard			
Lighting			
Fencing			
Energy efficiency			
Overall Exterior			
NEIGHBORHOOD			
Traffic			
Noise Level			
Safety/Security			
Number of Children			
Pet Restrictions			
Appearance of Nearby Homes			
Parking			
Zoning			
Fire Protection			
Police			
Snow Removal			
Garbage Service			
DISTANCE TO:			
Supermarket			
Work			
Schools			
Shopping			
Child Care			
Hospitals			
Doctor/Dentist			
Recreation/Parks			
Restaurants/ Entertainment			
Place of Worship			
Airport			
Highway			
Public Transportation			

4 All About Real Estate Brokers

Why go it alone when you're shopping for a home? More than 90% of all homebuyers use the services of a professional real estate broker. And there's a good reason for this: real estate brokers are housing specialists. They deal with the ins and outs of homebuying all day long. They can save you time and money—and their services rarely cost you anything! That's because the seller almost always pays the broker's commission. As the buyer, you're entitled to benefit from a broker's experience and expertise for free!

Look at it this way. You could waste hours driving around on your own, trying to find a property or two—or you could let someone who knows where all the properties are take you around, tell you about them, and lead you to other opportunities you never knew existed. That someone is a professional real estate broker!

Some of the affordable housing programs we talk about in this catalog—for example, the programs of HUD—actually require you to use a real estate broker. (HUD pays the broker's commission, too.) There's just no substitute for a good broker. Consider this:

- Brokers know the local market better than anyone else. They know what's available now, what homes have sold for in the recent past, and what properties are just about to come on the market.
- Brokers have contacts to other real estate professionals, such as appraisers and home inspectors, whose services you'll need during the homebuying process.

In your Foreclosed Property Listings, you'll sometimes find the names of brokers to contact for more information on a particular property. Other times the contact person will be the representative of a government agency. When the contact person is a broker, the easiest thing to do is to go ahead and work with them directly—especially if you don't have a broker of your own.

However, it's a smart move to find a broker you can work with right in your own town—someone who knows what you want and who'll be looking out for you in the weeks and months to come—someone who'll go to bat for you until you've got the keys to your new home in hand.

BUYER'S TIP:
Perhaps most important of all, a broker can help you structure the most favorable purchase contract on your home to save you money!

Finding the Right Broker

Of course, not EVERY broker will be right for you. So how do you find one? You can start out in the Yellow Pages of your phone book. Call various real estate offices and ask to speak with a broker who specializes in foreclosed properties and other affordable housing.

But the very best way is to get recommendations from your friends, family, neighbors, and anyone else you know who's bought a house recently. Call the broker and meet with them in person. Be sure you like them before you agree to let them be your broker!

BUYER'S TIP:
If you can, seek out a real estate broker who is a member of the National Association of REALTORS®. These brokers are professionally licensed and trained, and they follow a strict code of ethics. Call your local Board of REALTORS® for a referral.

Questions to Ask a Broker

Before you agree to work with a broker ask them questions like these:

- How long have you lived in the area?
- What is your background and expertise?
- Where have you sold houses recently?
- Do you specialize in foreclosed properties and other affordable housing?
- Can you show me letters of recommendation from satisfied clients?

Stand By Your Broker

Once you've found a broker you like, give them the privilege of being your exclusive representative. Let them help you check out the properties in your Foreclosed Property Listings and locate other similar properties that might not be listed yet.

Real estate brokers don't like it when you play the field. If you try to work with more than one broker at the same time, you're going to shoot yourself in the foot. When they find out, which they inevitably will, no one will want to work with you. So do the right thing—find a broker, and stick with him or her throughout your homebuying process!

BUYER'S TIP:
Are you moving to a new town? Some real estate brokers are relocation specialists. They'll direct you to the right neighborhoods, match you with the right home, and assist you with the buying process.

The Multiple Listing Service

By all means, choose a broker who has access to the Multiple Listing Service (MLS). Just about all brokers do, but always check to be sure. The MLS includes homes listed by all of its member agencies, which means you have access to a great many more homes than you would if you worked with a single real estate office.

A good broker will be familiar with MLS listings in your area and be able to show you homes that are listed by other agencies. That can be a valuable supplement to your Foreclosed Property Listings and any other listings you obtain from the agencies featured in this catalog.

Making the Offer

Another way your broker will help you is when it's time to make an offer. While only you can decide how much to offer, your broker has information on hand to help you make that decision—like the recent selling prices of other homes in the area. Your broker will also know how long the property has been listed and whether the seller has already lowered the original asking price.

BUYER'S TIP:
Keep in mind that your final contract on a home should allow you to do a walk-through inspection 24 hours prior to closing. You should have the option to delay the closing if you find any problems.

The broker will present your offer to the seller and return the answer to you. If the seller comes back with a counter offer, the broker will relay your response to them. And if your offer is accepted, the broker will handle the contract procedures and see the deal through, right up to the moment you sign the papers at closing.

So as you can see, a good real estate broker can be a valuable asset to your house-hunting efforts. Now turn to Chapter 5 and learn all about the next step on your pathway to home ownership—how to get a loan!

5 How To Get A Loan

Maybe you've never bought a home before because you thought you couldn't qualify for a mortgage. Or maybe you thought, "I don't have enough money for a down payment." Or if your credit is less than perfect, maybe you let that stop you.

Well the good news is, there are plenty of mortgage opportunities out there! And there are two different approaches you can follow to get your loan. Approach #1 is to read the information in this section on "How To Get A Loan." Just follow our step-by-step guidelines and you'll be well prepared to shop for a mortgage on your own. Approach #2 is far simpler: you can let us get you started right away! That's right! At Bargain Property Network, we can help you pre-qualify for a mortgage in just 24 hours, even if you have bad credit history! (Please see page 38 for exciting details.) Regardless of which mortgage shopping approach you choose, stay positive. Getting a mortgage in today's economy is a whole lot easier than you think!

MORTGAGE TIP:
We can help you pre-qualify for a mortgage in just 24 hours, even if you have bad credit history! Call 1-800-333-1915 now and we'll take your application right over the phone!

Start Mortgage Shopping Now!

If you've started shopping for a home, it's time to shop for a mortgage loan, too. All kinds of institutions offer affordable mortgages to buyers like yourself. You can choose from banks, savings and loans, credit unions, private mortgage companies, and the various government lenders we talk about in this book.

Ask your broker for the names of lenders to contact. If you're the do-it-yourself type, look in the Yellow Pages under "Mortgages" or check the real estate section of your

BUYER'S TIP:
Refer to Chapters 6 through 11 for information on the AMAZING affordable loan programs offered by government agencies!

local newspaper for lenders' ads and mortgage rate hotlines. Some lenders will do a computerized search for you for free!

You'll want to talk to at least three lenders and compare their rates and terms. That way you can find the best deal on a loan before you make an offer. Plus, pre-qualifying with a lender will speed up the loan process and eliminate problems that might come up later.

Use the Mortgage Comparison Chart on the next page to compare mortgages from different lenders. You can also use this chart to learn the different parts of a mortgage. Make a new copy of this chart for each lender you visit and fill in the blanks. Then you'll be able to see at a glance which lender offers the best deal for you!

Compare and Save

Shopping for a mortgage is like shopping for anything else: you'll save money if you look around for the best price. As you comparison shop for mortgages, you'll notice that the biggest differences between lenders occur in interest rates and loan fees, also known as closing costs. These fees are listed on the Mortgage Comparison Chart; they usually average 3% to 4% of your home's purchase price. Take the chart with you to each lender and write down the fees charged by each one.

By comparison shopping, you can save yourself thousands of dollars at closing, and even tens of thousands of dollars over the life of your loan. So just remember that the time you spend now visiting different lenders will be repaid many times over!

Mortgage Comparison Chart

Company Name: ____________________

Loan Officer: ____________________

Date Quoted: ____________________

Type of Mortgage: ____________________

Interest Rate: ____________________

Points: ____________________

Interest Rate Lock-Ins:

Upon application or upon approval? ____________________

Effective how long? ____________________

Lower lock-in if rates drop? ____________________

Lock-in costs? ____________________

Down Payment: ____________________

Prepayment of Principal:

Is prepayment allowed? ____________________

Is there a penalty? ____________________

Mortgage Insurance:

Upfront costs ____________________

Monthly premiums ____________________

Can it be financed? ____________________

Loan Processing Time:

Days from application to approval ____________________

Days from approval to closing ____________________

Closing Costs:

Application/origination fee ____________________

Credit report fee ____________________

Lender's attorney fee ____________________

Document preparation fee ____________________

Transfer taxes ____________________

Appraisal fee ____________________

Survey fee ____________________

Title search/title insurance ____________________

Other costs ____________________

The Relationship Between Interest Rates and Points

BUYER'S TIP:
Many agencies and loan programs will help you out with closing costs. For example, HUD will pay your closing costs for you! For more information, see Chapter 8.

As you become savvy about loans, you'll notice that there's a close relationship between interest rates and points. A point (also known as a "discount point") is an upfront fee charged by your lender which equals 1% of your loan amount. The more points you pay, the lower your interest rate will be over the life of your loan.

To help you get the idea, ask your lender for an interest rate on a loan with no points at all. Then ask for the rate on a loan with one or more points. You'll see the difference in the interest rate—AND monthly payments—right away!

Keep in mind that points are paid at closing, which means you need more cash up front. However, you can sometimes negotiate with the seller to pay some points on your loan—and many loan programs will also help with these costs.

BUYER'S TIP:
Interest rates change frequently, so you may want to ask your mortgage lender to offer you a rate lock-in that will guarantee you a low interest rate.

Remember that you only pay points once, but the interest rate is with you for the entire term of the loan. So, if you can afford it, get a loan with up-front points and keep your interest rate, and mortgage payments, as low as possible!

Types of Mortgages

• **Fixed-Rate Mortgage.** With this mortgage, your interest rate and monthly payments never change for the entire length, or term, of the mortgage. Usually this type of mortgage has a term of 30 years. Sometimes you can get a fixed-rate mortgage for 25, 20, or even 15 years. The 30-year mortgage is the easiest to qualify for. The advantage is that your monthly payments are low and you can use the extra cash for other purposes.

• **Adjustable-Rate Mortgage (ARM).** ARMS are very popular these days, because your interest rate and monthly payments start out lower than a fixed-rate mortgage. However, your interest rate later goes up or down depending on what's happening with a national financial index; the three most commonly used are the Treasury Index, CD Index, and Cost of Funds Index. Your monthly payments will also go up at regular intervals, usually once or twice a year for a certain number of years. ARMS have "caps" that keep your monthly payment and interest rate from changing too much over the life of the loan. Some ARMS allow you to convert to a fixed-rate loan within a certain period of time—a smart move if interest rates drop during the first years of your ARM!

• **Two-Step Mortgage.** This is an ARM that adjusts only once, at either five or seven years. After that, the mortgage remains at a fixed rate for the rest of its life. You get the benefits of a low starting interest rate and the stability of a fixed rate over time.

• **Balloon Mortgage.** With this type of mortgage, you get a fixed monthly payment and low interest rates for the first five, seven, or ten years of the loan. At the end of that time the entire balance is due in one lump sum. Balloon mortgages are great if you plan to move in a few years and sell the home—or, if you plan to refinance in a few years. Sometimes you can extend the loan by paying a fee and refinancing at the prevailing interest rate. The risk of a balloon mortgage comes if you plan on keeping the home indefinitely. Then you must either pay the balance in full on the agreed-upon date or refinance at a different (and possibly higher) interest rate.

• **Government-Insured Mortgages.** These loans are perfect for folks who can't afford to make a 10% to 20% down payment on a home. With a government-insured mortgage, you can put down as little as 3%. Agencies that offer these mortgages are the FHA (Federal Housing Administration—

see Chapter 8); VA (Department of Veterans Affairs—see Chapter 10); and RECDS (Rural Economic and Community Development Services—see Chapter 11).

BUYER'S TIP

Often you'll find a home with a loan that you can take over, or "assume," from the previous owner. Many of these loans are great bargains, with low interest rates and low montly payments. Be sure to compare interest rates and payments on these assumable loans with rates available to you on new loans.

• **Fannie Mae and Freddie Mac Mortgages.** These two government-supported institutions both offer great loan programs that allow you to put as little as 3% down with low monthly payments. See Chapters 6 and 7 in this catalog for details.

A Word About Prequalifying

Prequalifying is a chance to learn exactly how much mortgage money a lender will offer you. There's no obligation and you benefit by getting a ballpark range of your buying power.

As a rule of thumb, you can figure on borrowing up to 2-1/2 times your gross annual household income. But with the special government programs available to you, you can probably borrow even more than that! You'll never know, though, until you sit down with a lender and run through the figures. We recommend you do so as soon as possible!

Before you sit down with a lender, write down your total monthly income before taxes and your total monthly debts. There are three items lenders will look at when you go to apply for a mortgage:

• **Your job history.** Lenders like to see steady employment, which shows you can keep up with your monthly mortgage payments. If you've been working continuously for two years or more, you're considered to have steady employment. That doesn't mean you need to have worked at the same job—you can change jobs, and as long as you have equal or greater money coming in. There ARE exceptions to this rule, such as if you were recently discharged from the military, or if your work is seasonal.

• **Your credit history.** If you pay your bills on time every month, it will help you get a mortgage loan. Lenders will ask you to list all your debts, the amount of your monthly payments, and how much longer until your debts are paid off. Then the lender will order a copy of your credit report to verify this information. If you are late on payments or owe too much, the lender may want you to pay off some debts and get up to date on your payments before granting a mortgage.

If you've never had a credit card or taken out a loan, you may not have a credit report on file. If not, you can use a "nontraditional" credit history, which includes records of how you've paid your rent, telephone bills, or utility bills on time every month.

• **Your savings.** Lenders will want to know if you have any money saved for a down payment and closing costs. Remember, with the special loan programs available to you, your down payment can be as low as 3% to 5%, and there are many options to help you pay closing costs. See the affordable housing programs described in Chapters 6-11 for details.

BUYER'S TIP:
"Underwriting" is the term used to describe the process by which the lender reviews all the information about you and your loan, including the value of the property and your ability to repay the loan.

BUYER'S TIP:
Sometimes there are errors on credit reports. To check the accuracy of your credit report, you can order a copy for free or for a small fee from a credit reporting agency. See your local Yellow Pages under "Credit Reporting Agencies."

Loan Application Information

You will need the following information on hand when you go to fill out a loan application:

- Your home addresses for the past seven years
- The names, addresses and phone numbers of your employers for the past two years.
- Two recent pay stubs and your W-2 forms for the past two years. If you are self-employed, you will need to submit the past two years' tax returns.
- If you receive alimony and child support, you will need to bring copies of your divorce decree and court documents ordering these payments.
- The balances, account numbers, and names and addresses of the institutions where your savings, checking, and investment accounts are located.
- The names and addresses of all your creditors plus account numbers, current balances, and monthly payments.
- The sources of money for your down payment.

We Can Help You Obtain a Mortgage in 24 Hours!

Bargain Property Network can help you pre-qualify for a mortgage in as little as 24 hours even if you have a bad or no credit history! Simply call our friendly customer support department at **(877) 385-5107** and tell them you want to apply for a mortgage by phone.

In a few short minutes, we can take down the information that's necessary for you to obtain a home loan. Then, we transmit your completed loan application electronically to one or more leading mortgage providers, who start working on your loan right away! Because we use high-speed digital technology, in most cases, you'll have a loan decision in as little as 24 hours.

And because our loan providers understand that not everyone has perfect credit, there's an excellent chance we can help you find a great mortgage regardless of your past credit history. So what are you waiting for? Grab your phone and call **(877) 385-5107**. Let's get you pre-approved for your mortgage right now!

Should I Refinance My Existing Mortgage?

If you own an existing home and wish to keep it for a while, it probably makes sense for you to refinance your old mortgage at today's rock-bottom interest rates! Many people reduce their mortgage payment by hundreds of dollars each month when they refinance at today's incredible low rates. Bargain Property Network can help you obtain a new, low interest mortgage that will replace your old, higher interest loan! We'll take your loan information right over the phone and electronically transmit your application to one or more leading loan providers. In most cases, you'll have loan pre-approval in just 24 hours! So call us today at 1-800-333-1915. Lower monthly mortgage payments are just a phone call away!

6 Fannie Mae Loans

If you're in the market for a home loan, rest assured that Fannie Mae will bend over backwards to help you! This organization, which was originally known as the Federal National Mortgage Association, has been in existence for over 50 years. Today Fannie Mae is the nation's largest source of home mortgage funds. In fact, Fannie Mae is committed to provide *$1 trillion* in affordable housing loans by the year 2000 to the following special groups:

- Low and moderate-income families
- Minorities
- New immigrants
- Residents of central cities and other underserved areas
- Other people with special housing needs

Fannie Mae's slogan is "Showing America A New Way Home." It's a government-backed, private company that provides mortgage money to local banks, savings and loans, credit unions, and mortgage companies all across America. All you have to do is go to the lending institution of your choice for a home loan—no matter who you pick, chances are they have Fannie Mae money on hand to make you a loan.

This chapter will show you how to take advantage of the home loan opportunities offered by Fannie Mae—plus the many outstanding educational opportunities offered to home buyers by this great institution.

Ready, Set, Dial!

The first step is to request Fannie Mae's informative home buyer's guide, *Opening the Door to a Home of Your Own*. You may have heard of this publication from the many TV ads run by Fannie Mae in 1995. To order this FREE booklet, all you do is call 1-800-688-4663. Do it today! (By the way, this booklet is available in English, Spanish, Korean, Chinese, and Vietnamese.)

At the same time you ask for the booklet, you can also request lists of mortgage lending institutions in your area that are ready to work with you.

Not only that—Fannie Mae will also send a list of home buyer education providers in your area who will help you figure out exactly how to turn your dream of home ownership into reality. Armed with this information, you'll be ready to tackle the challenges of homebuying head-on!

Fannie Mae's HomePath[sm] Program

Remember Fannie Mae's commitment to making $1 trillion in affordable housing loans that we mentioned at the beginning of this chapter? To achieve that goal, Fannie Mae has created HomePath, a nationwide home buyer referral and guidance service.

HomePath is designed to break down barriers to information and put more individuals than ever before on the path to home ownership. It's a FREE service designed to help anyone who needs personal assistance in preparing for home ownership—and that's just about everyone!

To speak to a Fannie Mae HomePath specialist, call 1-800-832-2345. You will receive the names of any organizations in your area that provide free advice on the home buying process—plus your Fannie Mae HomePath specialist will give you direct guidance over the telephone. You also have the option of taking Fannie Mae's award-winning home study course called *Guide to Homeownership.*

Get In the Know!

Here's a plug for Fannie Mae's home study course, the *Guide to Homeownership*. The easy-to-follow course walks you step-by-step through the entire home buying process. As you go through the course, you will complete five worksheets which are then reviewed by your HomePath specialist at no cost to you!

When you've finished this free course, you will receive a certificate showing that you've satisfied the education requirement for Fannie Mae's Community Home Buyer's Program. This program makes it even easier for you to participate in special Fannie Mae financing opportunities. You'll find more details on the Community Home Buyer's Program on the next page.

By the time you've completed the *Guide to Homeownership*, you'll be confident and knowledgeable about your options—even if you've never bought a home before!

BUYER'S TIP:
Fannie Mae's HomePath services are available in English, Spanish, and other languages as well. Ask for details when you call 1-800-832-2345.

Desktop Home Counselor

How would you like a FREE in-depth review of your financial situation? That's exactly what you'll get from Fannie Mae's Desktop Home Counselor. This service combines a review of your credit report with details of your current financial picture. After analyzing this information, the Desktop Home Counselor will give you examples of home ownership options you can use right away! Plus, a HomePath specialist will work with you through the entire homebuying process. To find out more, call 1-800-832-2345. Or log onto **www.homepath.com/hpc2.html** for a handy calculator and worksheet.

Fannie Mae Regional Programs

Fannie Mae currently has special regional home buyer's programs underway in the following areas: El Paso, Texas; Laredo, Texas; New Orleans, Louisiana; and the state

BUYER'S TIP:
If you are interested in Fannie Mae loans or mortgage programs, please call customer support at 1-800-333-1915.

of Minnesota. To receive an information packet about these programs, call the Fannie Mae Public Information Office at 1-800-732-6643 and select Option 1 on the phone menu.

More regional homebuying programs may be available soon in other areas of the country, so call the 800 number listed above every few months to see if a program has been established in your area.

Power Mortgage Shopping

Ready to shop for a mortgage? Fannie Mae has an easy-to-read, 40-page guide that's just for you. It's called *Choosing the Mortgage That's Right For You,* and it breaks down the mortgage shopping process into three steps:

- Discovering how big a mortgage loan you can afford
- Choosing a mortgage that's right for you
- Comparing terms among lenders

This guide includes worksheets that help you calculate your mortgage buying power; checklists to remind you of important questions to ask lenders; and discussions of the various types of mortgages. You'll learn all about interest rates, repayment terms, down payments, and closing costs.

To send for your FREE guide, call Fannie Mae at 1-800-688-HOME (1-800-688-4663). It's available in both English and Spanish.

Community Home Buyer's Program

Fannie Mae's Community Home Buyer's Program (CHBP) can help you if:

- You have trouble coming up with enough money for a down payment.
- Your monthly income isn't high enough to qualify for a regular mortgage.
- Your lender says you have too much debt to qualify

The Community Home Buyer's Program offers loans that require less income to qualify and less cash for a down payment than standard conventional loans. Also, the program offers home buyer education courses through lenders in your area that will give you great advice on choosing a home, obtaining a mortgage, budgeting to meet monthly expenses, and home maintenance.

Your purchasing power takes a quantum leap with the CHBP. You can borrow up to $203,150! And if you want to buy a home in Alaska or Hawaii, you can borrow up to $304,725. Now that's something to write home about!

What Can You Buy?

The Community Home Buyer's Program exists specifically to help you buy a single-family home, townhouse, or condominium. You must plan to make this home your primary residence. It does not matter whether your future home is new, previously owned, or rehabilitated.

The Median is the Message

Incredibly enough, there is only one basic requirement to participate in the CHBP: your household income must be no more than 100% of the median household income in the area where you want to buy. Remember, median household income means that half the households in the area earn more than you, and the other half earns less.

There ARE exceptions to this requirement if you live in the high-cost areas listed below:

- In the State of California, you can earn up to 120% of the area median income.
- In the State of Hawaii, you can earn up to 170% of the area median income.
- In the New York City metropolitan area, you can earn up to 165% of the median income.
- In the Boston metropolitan area, you can earn up to 120% of the area median income.

The income limit can be waived if you buy a home in a designated central city. There are hundreds of these cities all across the country, and all areas within the city limits are included! See Appendix C of this catalog for a list of designated central cities. For more information, see the section on FannieNeighbors® later in this chapter.

CHBP Benefits

Under the Community Home Buyer's Program, you can buy a home with a down payment as low as 5%. You can then choose a 15-year to 30-year fixed-rate mortgage loan. You can borrow up to 95% of the appraised value or sales price of the home, whichever is less.

While the program prefers that your down payment money comes from your own savings, a special option allows family members, nonprofit groups, and public agencies to step in and pay some of your closing costs and down payment. This can be a real lifesaver!

The CHBP allows you to use up to 33% of your gross monthly income for housing expenses and up to 38% of your gross monthly income for your total debt obligations. Finally, the program waives the usual requirement for "cash reserves"; with a conventional mortgage, you are usually required to have two months of mortgage payments saved up in addition to your down payment and closing costs.

All these benefits add up to super savings for you, and can make the difference between getting a home of your own or just playing the renting game for years to come!

More Loans for People with Limited Resources

Under the umbrella of the Community Home Buyer's Program (CHBP), there are four additional options for qualified homebuyers:

• Fannie 97sm. This loan is perfect if you have enough money to handle the monthly mortgage payments but don't have quite enough for the down payment. With Fannie 97, you just need 3% down from your own funds, and you can borrow up to 97% of the appraised value or sales price of the house, whichever is less. You have your choice of a 25-year or 30-year fixed-rate mortgage.

• CHBP with the 3/2 Option. The 3/2 Option is another way of getting more flexibility when it comes to your down payment. It allows you to provide just 3% of the down payment from your own funds, and 2% from other sources —a gift, a grant, an unsecured loan from a nonprofit organization, a public agency. The 3/2 Option is available for 15- to 30-year fixed-rate mortgages. You can borrow up to 95% of the appraised value or sales price of the house, whichever is less.

• CHBP Start-Up Mortgagesm. This is the program for you if your income is best described as "modest." What you get is a 30-year fixed-rate graduated payment mortgage. During the first year of the mortgage, your payments are lower than normal because they consist only of interest, which makes it easier for you to qualify. After the first year, your monthly payment increases by 2% each year for the next four to eight years until the maximum monthly payment is reached. You must put up a 5% down payment from your own funds, and you can borrow up to 95% of the appraised value or sales price of the house, whichever is less.

• Fannie Neighbors®. This program removes the standard median income limits if you buy your home in a designated central city or an eligible census tract. For a list of designated central cities, see Appendix C in this catalog. For the eligible census tracts near you, contact your local Community Home Buyer's Program mortgage lender. Call customer support, 1-800-333-1915, to see if you can be pre-approved for a mortgage loan.

7 Freddie Mac REOs and Loans

Freddie Mac—also known as the Federal Home Loan Mortgage Corporation, or FHLMC—is a private corporation that was chartered by Congress in 1970. Since that time it has financed more than $1 trillion worth of mortgage loans. In fact, one out of every six homes in America is purchased with financing made possible by Freddie Mac!

In the 1990s, Freddie Mac has a mandate to reach out to borrowers who have experienced difficulty entering the traditional mortgage market. *Low-income, minority, rural, and inner-city borrowers are at the top of the list!* Pilot programs are now under way in different parts of the country to make more mortgages than ever available to these individuals.

What Freddie Mac does is push the envelope of traditional mortgage requirements to help more people qualify. For example, if you have reasonably good credit but not enough money for a down payment, your lender can still qualify you with the help of Freddie Mac.

If your credit is less than perfect, there's still hope! Freddie Mac encourages lenders to take an understanding look at your total credit history. Call Customer Support toll-free a 1-800-333-1915 to find out if you can pre-qualify for a mortgage loan.

Freddie Mac REOs

Along with helping people at all income levels get home loans, Freddie Mac has its very own inventory of REO properties, accumulated when people default on Freddie Mac mortgages. In your Foreclosed Property Listings, these

Freddie Mac properties are identified under the agency's other name—as FHLMC properties.

Freddie Mac REOs are sold through local real estate brokers. The contact names are listed on your Foreclosed Property Listings and on any lists you obtain from Freddie Mac itself. If you already have your own broker, have them call the contact name and arrange to show you the property. Your broker can obtain the latest information on the status of any Freddie Mac properties in your area—all you have to do is ask!

For a complete list of Freddie Mac REOs in your state, call Freddie Mac Customer Service toll-free at 1-800-972-7555.

When you talk to the agent, leave your name and address to receive the property list you want. Or visit the HOMESTEPS website, **www.homesteps.com/gsearch.html** where you will find a convenient geographic search tool that will help you search for the home in your area.

How Freddie Mac Works

You may not have heard of Freddie Mac before because it does not make loans directly to you, the home buyer. Instead, it buys up mortgages from lenders like your local bank. It then packages those mortgages as securities and sells them to investors.

This process creates a continuous flow of new money into the home mortgage market. That means more money for mortgages, and better mortgage opportunities for people like you.

No Loan Too Small

Freddie Mac is fond of saying that "no loan is too small." That means when lenders ordinarily would say "no" to your application for a mortgage, Freddie Mac gives them the backing they need to say "yes." Here are the ways

Freddie Mac helps lenders to improve the affordable housing market.

- There is no minimum loan size—Freddie Mac will back up almost any loan.
- Loans are available all across the country, including hard-to-finance locations like rural areas and inner cities.
- Lenders are required to qualify buyers on a case-by-case basis—exceptions are the rule!
- When you list your income to qualify, you can boost the total by including part-time earnings, unemployment compensation, and public assistance.

BUYER'S TIP:
Still confused about Freddie Mac? Freddie Mac explains it like this: pretend your local mortgage lender is a store where you go to buy a mortgage. Freddie Mac is the *supplier* where your lender gets the money to sell you a mortgage.

Talk to Your Lender

As you know by now, opportunity knocks when you go looking for it. And in the case of Freddie Mac loan assistance, the best approach is to ask your local bank, savings and loan, or other lender about Freddie Mac options. These are described in detail in the sections below. As you will see, Freddie Mac really goes to bat for you!

Lowdown on Down Payments

Under Freddie Mac rules, the money you need for a down payment and closing costs can come from a variety of sources, including the following:

- Grants from municipalities and nonprofit community organizations. You'll be amazed to learn that these grants *don't have to be repaid!*
- Rental/purchase agreements. You live in the property you want to buy and pay extra rent each month, which is credited towards the down payment. When the agreement is up, the rent credits form the *entire* down payment.
- Pooled funds. If you have an extended family that

will all be living in the same house, multiple family members can contribute money towards the down payment.

- Grace period. If you're just shy of the funds you need for closing, you can make up the difference during the time the loan is being processed.

BUYER'S TIP:
Ask about Freddie Mac's Affordable Gold Program, which now has a 3/2 option allowing you to put 3% down with an additional 2% down coming from gifts, grants, or other sources.

Loans for People with Imperfect Credit

With the support of Freddie Mac, lenders can be more flexible in accommodating buyers with less-than-perfect credit. Freddie Mac asks lenders to look at your overall payment history rather than penalizing you for a few late payments. Freddie Mac recognizes that special circumstances can cause you to have late payments, and does not think that should keep you from qualifying for a mortgage.

The same is true if you have less-than-stable employment. If you have changed jobs frequently, lenders ordinarily might not approve your application. But Freddie Mac asks lenders to give more weight to stable income than to stable employment. In other words, as long as your income has maintained at about the same level for the past two or three years, you're all set.

In addition, stable income is allowed to come from a variety of sources, not just your job—alimony, child support, public assistance, nontaxable income, and retirement funds all qualify as income. The only restriction is that the income must be verified and reasonably expected to continue for the next three years.

Survival of the Fittest

Freddie Mac and Fannie Mae are both private companies backed by the Federal government, and they are strong competitors—both going after your mortgage dollars. In the best tradition of American free enterprise, the competition between them keeps mortgage costs low—and keeps Americans the best-housed people in the world.

Some lenders may deal with Fannie Mae only, some with Freddie Mac, and some with both. When you are shopping for a home loan, do just like you do when buying any other big-ticket item—compare and save! Since your home will probably be the biggest purchase you make in your life, the extra time you put in now in shopping for a loan will be time well spent.

BUYER'S TIP:
Look for an energy-efficient home—meaning, one with weather-stripping, double-paned windows, and the like. Why? Your utility costs will be less, and as a result your lender will let your monthly mortgage payment be that much more—thanks to the support of Freddie Mac.

The Half-Percent Halo

Along with creating better access to home financing, both Fannie Mae and Freddie Mac's programs result in lower monthly payments for you. You can usually save up to one-half of one percent on your mortgage rate. Unimpressed? Don't be. That one-half of one percent will save you thousands and thousands of dollars over the life of your mortgage.

Community Development Mortgage Lending

This lending program of Freddie Mac provides financing for both owner-occupied and rental housing in certain geographic areas. Eligible properties must qualify as affordable housing for low, moderate, or middle-income households.

The ultimate goal of this program is to build stronger neighborhoods. Freddie Mac creates partnerships with public, private, philanthropic, and community-based organizations to make it happen. One example of this program is called NeighborWorks®, which provides grassroots lending for affordable housing. Another example is the American Dream Program sponsored by the Massachusetts Housing Finance Agency.

New programs are being added all the time, so you may be able to find one in your state. Call Freddie Mac toll-free at 1-800-373-3343 for the latest, up-to-date information on these special housing options for you!

8 Affordable Housing from HUD

The Department of Housing and Urban Development (HUD) is dedicated to bringing home ownership within the reach of just about everyone. Since 1934, HUD has helped millions of Americans realize the dream of home ownership. It's one of the most important resources that you, the prospective home buyer, can use to find affordable housing.

So why aren't HUD Homes included on your Foreclosed Property Listings? Because HUD does not publish lists of the properties it has for sale, nor does it make this information available to other agencies.

There are a few ways you can find out about HUD Homes on the market in your area: read the real estate section of your local newspaper (some, but not all, will carry HUD listings); work with a real estate broker who participates in the HUD Homes sales program; check out **www.hud.gov**; or visit one of HUD's interactive "next door kiosks" (listed in Appendix A where applicable). HUD offices also have a computer where the public can access the internet. It's also a smart move to contact your local HUD office directly—see Appendix A of this catalog for a complete list of HUD offices nationwide.

This chapter will explain the workings of the HUD Homes sales program and what it can do for you—plus we'll talk about the great financing opportunities available to you through HUD's FHA-insured mortgage program.

Get Brokered

HUD requires you to work with a real estate broker, so the first thing you want to do is find a broker who handles HUD homes. How to do this? One way is to check the real estate section of your local newspaper. Some brokers advertise that they sell HUD homes.

BUYER'S TIP:
The good news is, HUD pays the broker's commission, which allows you to take advantage of the vast knowledge, experience, and resources of a broker *at no cost to you!*

If you don't find someone in the paper, just call around to a few local real estate offices and ask for a broker who specializes in HUD homes. There are LOTS of brokers who handle HUD properties, so don't worry—you'll be able to find someone right away!

Brokers are on the inside track when it comes to HUD homes. Every broker that participates in the HUD Homes program gets several faxes a month from HUD with all the latest property listings in your area. The only way to hook up with this inside information is to get yourself a broker.

Where Do HUD Homes Come From?

An explanation of HUD homes must include an explanation of the FHA, or Federal Housing Administration. The FHA offers insured mortgages on homes. When FHA-insured homes go into foreclosure, someone has to pay the balance due on the mortgage—and that someone is HUD. Then HUD turns around and sells these REO properties to buyers like yourself.

HUD homes include single-family homes, townhomes, condominiums, 2-4 unit residences, and more. HUD must sell these homes quickly to get the maximum return on its investment. While HUD tries to sell its homes at fair market value, the truth of the matter is that they often sell for far less! And even at fair market value, HUD offers so many incentives to buyers interested in affordable housing that it's hard to pass up these deals. Read on for details.

Affordable Housing Heaven

HUD homes are like manna from heaven if you're looking for affordable housing. Here's a quick checklist of how buying a HUD home saves you money:

- HUD homes often require a down payment of only 3%. *Some HUD homes can be had for as little as $100 down!*
- HUD pays the real estate broker's commission, up to 6% of the sales price.
- HUD often pays the closing costs, allowing you to get into a HUD home for less cash than other homes.

BUYER'S TIP:
HUD REOs are perfect for people with little or no down payment. Many require only 3% down, while some can be had for just $100 dollars down!

Low Income Myths

HUD has such a strong reputation for selling homes to low-income buyers that some people think you HAVE to be a low-income buyer to purchase a HUD home. Not so! HUD homes come in a variety of price ranges, and anyone who has the money can buy a HUD home—there are no income restrictions.

Investors can buy HUD homes too, though usually HUD offers its homes to owner/occupants for a fixed period of time first. If they don't sell within a set period of time, investors are then allowed to step in.

HUD Fixer-Uppers

It will probably be no surprise to you that the best deals on HUD homes are on fixer-uppers—but you just might be surprised at how good these deals can be! How about a 4-bedroom, 2-bath home with a fireplace, central air conditioning, and a swimming pool for $70,000—in a neighborhood where the average home price is $120,000? This is a perfect example of the ultimate fixer-upper: a home in a good neighborhood that needs just a little TLC to be worth far more than you paid for it!

HUD often lowers the prices on these homes to take into account the costs of making any necessary improvements. The catch with HUD homes is that no guarantees are offered regarding their condition. What you see, and what you DON'T see, is what you get. So it's more than a good idea—it's a necessity!—to get a professional inspection done on any HUD home you're seriously thinking about buying.

BUYER'S TIP:
HUD can lend you the money to make the improvements on a fixer-upper as part of an FHA-insured financing program called the 203(k). This program allows you to repay the cost of repairs as part of your mortgage. Not all homes in all areas are part of this program, so check with your broker about this great HUD opportunity.

The Sealed Bid Scene

For years, HUD homes have been sold through local real estate brokers by the sealed bid process. The home goes on the market—you have one chance to submit a bid—and you either win or lose, that's that.

If you are interested in a property, your broker will take you out to see it and guide you through the process of placing a bid. There is usually a 10-day "Offer Period" during which all bids on a property must be made. Your broker will submit the offer for you. At the end of the 10-day period, all the bids are opened at a public event. Full price offers, if any, are opened first. While you are welcome to attend, you don't have to be present to "win"; your broker will be notified within 48 hours.

An earnest money deposit is required along with your offer. If your offer is accepted, this deposit becomes part of your down payment. If your offer is rejected, your earnest money is, of course, returned.

This is the traditional method of selling HUD homes, and it's still going strong. However, another sales method is now taking the nation by storm . . .

HUD Open Auctions

In recent years, HUD is starting to sell its homes at open auction in some parts of the country. Why? The housing market hasn't been good, and HUD has a backlog of unsold properties. Open auctions allow HUD to sell hundreds of properties at a single sale—and the selling prices are the lowest you'll find anywhere on HUD homes!

Here are the advantages of HUD open-bid auctions:

- The standard down payment is 3%.
- Some homes are FHA-insured.
- HUD pays the broker's 3% commission, plus deed preparation costs and other charges up to another 3%.
- Rock-bottom purchase prices!

BUYER'S TIP:
HUD holds free Buyer Awareness Seminars before open auctions that cover everything you need to know about bidding, financing, and closing procedures. Ask your broker for details, and be sure to attend!

The best way to find out about HUD open-bid auctions is through a knowledgeable real estate broker. The advantage is you can start out bidding low and keep raising your price until you reach your limit—unlike the sealed bid auctions, where you have just one shot at success.

Probably the only danger of these open-bid auctions is that you might be tempted to bid more than you can really afford for a property. The secret is to decide the absolute maximum amount you can pay before you walk into the auction—and then stick to that decision, no matter what. Auctions pros always say that there's plenty more deals where that one came from—and that patience is rewarded at auctions. We think that's good advice!

Open Auction Procedures

Properties are usually open for inspection 10 days before the sale. It is NOT a good idea to rely on catalog pictures to make your decision. Remember that HUD properties are sold "as is," with no warranties or guarantees of any kind. There may be zoning and code violations as well as repairs that need to be done. The only way you'll know about these things is to visit the property yourself. And take your broker with you!

Why Work With A Broker?

Not all HUD open-bid auctions require you to work with a broker. You might think you can save more money by not using one—but wait just a minute! HUD pays the broker's commission anyway, and brokers provide you with an invaluable service by walking you through the entire home-buying process.

Choose a broker who knows the area you want to buy in. The broker will know what homes in that area are worth and will advise you on the maximum amount to pay for a property.

On Auction Day

Plan on attending an open auction with your broker. You'll need to bring the following:

- A letter from a HUD-approved lender, saying that you are prequalified for a certain mortgage amount. (See Chapter 5 for details.)
- $1,000 in earnest money—either cash, a cashier's check, or other form of certified funds. You'll forfeit this money if escrow fails to close, so be sure that you're in earnest!

When you register at the auction, you'll receive a

bidding card which you raise in the air to make your bids. At a big auction, a new property will go up on the auction block every couple of minutes. If you place the winning bid, you and your broker retire to the "contract room," where you complete the contract on the spot. There is usually a brief escrow, and then you're a happy homeowner!

FHA-Insured Mortgages

The magic words "3% Down" are what you'll hear when you apply for an FHA-insured mortgage. This program was created specifically to help homebuyers who can't afford the 10% to 20% down payment required by conventional lenders.

With FHA-insured loans, the Federal Government insures the loan against default. FHA-insured mortgages are open to both first-time buyers and people who have owned homes in the past. Sometimes the down payment figure can be even less than 3%!

The maximum FHA-insured mortgage amount is generally stated as being $67,500; however, in many areas where housing costs are high, this limit may be extended as high as $151,725. See Appendix A in this catalog, HUD Field Offices, and inquire about the mortgage limits for your area by calling the office nearest you.

FHA-Insured Mortgage Programs

- **Section 203(b) Home Mortgage Insurance**

This is the most widely used HUD program. It's available nationwide and you can use it to purchase a single family home, duplex, triplex, or fourplex. Loan repayment terms range from 10 to 30 years.

- **Section 234(c) Condominium Units**

  This is the program you want if you're interested in purchasing a condominium. HUD must approve the condominium project before you can use this program as part of your financing. The main requirement is that over 50% of the units in the project must be owner-occupied.

- **Section 203(k) Rehabilitation Home Mortgage Insurance**

  This mortgage enables you to purchase and repair a home. The only restriction is that the home must be at least one year old. The portion of the loan slated for repairs is held in an escrow account and paid out as the repairs are made.

  You can use this type of loan for additional purposes, as follows:

  - To move a home from one site to another and then repair it.
  - To refinance an existing mortgage in order to rehabilitate the home.
  - To convert non-residential buildings to residential buildings.
  - To add to the number of family units in a home.

- **Section 245(a) Graduated Payment Mortgage**

  This mortgage, known as a GPM, allows you to make lower payments during the first years you have the loan. The assumption is that your income is going to increase, and as it does, your loan payments also increase. Then they level off and remain steady for the remainder of the mortgage. Deferred interest from the early years is added to the loan balance in later years.

  There are five GPM plans offered by the FHA. The most popular is Plan 3, during which payments increase 7.5% each year for the first five years of the loan. After that point, the payments remain level for the term of the loan.

See the table below for an example of Plan 3 monthly payments:

Year 1	400.22/month
Year 2	430.24/month
Year 3	462.50/month
Year 4	497.20/month
Year 5	534.49/month
Year 6 on	574.57/month

BUYER'S TIP:
There are no upper age limits for borrowers seeking FHA-insured mortgages. So even if you are on the verge of retirement, you may be able to qualify for long-term mortgage.

- **Section 245(a) Growing Equity Mortgage**

Known as a GEM, this mortgage allows you to pay off your principal quickly and decrease the length of your mortgage term by increasing the amount of your payments over a period of time. The increase in your monthly payments is applied directly to the principal, which allows you to pay off the loan sooner—saving you a significant amount of money in the process!

- **Section 251 Adjustable Rate Mortgage (ARM)**

With an ARM, the monthly payment can either increase or decrease over the life of the loan. The initial interest rate will be in effect for the first 12 to 18 months, at which point the rate will be adjusted up or down depending what's happening with the one-year Treasury Index.

In any one year, your interest rate cannot fluctuate more than 1%. Over the entire life of the loan, the interest rate cannot go up or down more than 5%. These safeguards protect both you and the lender from excessive losses.

V-Day for Veterans

If you are a veteran seeking an FHA-insured mortgage to buy a single-family home, you are eligible to receive special terms from HUD. All you have to do is present your Certificate of Veterans Status from the Department of Veterans Affairs. Ask your local HUD office for details on this procedure. There is no limit on the number of times you can take advantage of your special status, so go for it!

Questions? Call Your Broker

Ask your broker for the details about FHA-insured loans. As we mentioned earlier in this chapter, there are some HUD homes that do not qualify for this program. Examples would be homes in very poor condition, homes that have fallen out of escrow more than once, and homes in neighborhoods with an epidemic of foreclosures.

Don't forget, though, that even if a HUD home does not qualify for the FHA-insured mortgage program, you can still buy it with a loan from a conventional lender. Enlist your broker's help in thoroughly investigating any HUD home that interests you. You'll find that HUD is more than willing to go the extra mile to make the sale.

A Final Note: Leaded Vs. Unleaded

For years HUD has led the crusade to increase public awareness about lead-based paint in American homes. Lead-based paint is a real health hazard for young children, who can be poisoned by chewing or teething on any surface that contains this toxic substance. Any home built before 1978 is suspect.

When you buy a HUD home, you must submit a form called a "lead-based paint addendum" along with your offer to buy the property. This is HUD's way of making sure you and your family know the risks of lead-based paint.

If lead-based paint does exist in the home you want to buy, it CAN be removed—for a price. Be sure you know the costs and make a decision about whether to go through with the process before you sign on the dotted line.

9 REOs and Loans from the FDIC

The Federal Deposit Insurance Corporation (FDIC) dates back to the Great Depression. It was founded in 1933 to restore public confidence at a time when many banks had failed. Today the FDIC provides peace of mind by insuring your deposits at banks throughout the nation—and when modern-day banks fail, the FDIC takes over and disposes of their assets. That means real estate bargains for you!

The FDIC sells all types of property: residential, multi-family, retail, office, industrial, land, hotel, and specialty properties. The FDIC focuses their marketing efforts on advertising in local and regional newspapers, and their internet site. On their web site, the FDIC lists properties available, has a searchable database (by property type, location and price), and lists frequently asked questions. Their listings are updated weekly (every Monday). Their internet site address is: **www.fdic.gov**. Select "Real Estate Sales" under "Buying from, Selling to FDIC."

The Resolution Trust Corporation (RTC) transferred operations to the FDIC on December 31, 1995. For further information regarding RTC properties, just contact the FDIC in your region.

When You Call

The Foreclosed Property Listings included with this catalog include the phone numbers and contact names for many FDIC properties. The contact person will either be an independent broker or a member of the FDIC sales staff. This person will send you an information package on the property you're interested in. It will include the terms and conditions of sale, procedures for making an offer, and the sales and purchase agreement.

BUYER'S TIP:
The cap on appraised housing values varies in different parts of the country. In some regions it may be $101,250 for a single-family home, while in other regions it may be as low as $60,000. Ask the regional FDIC Affordable Housing Coordinator about the cap in your area. (See the list of FDIC regional offices on the following page.)

Affordable Housing Program

The FDIC has a great Affordable Housing Program which sets aside certain residential properties for exclusive purchase by low and moderate income buyers. To be eligible, these properties must be appraised at an amount less than or equal to the FHA mortgage loan limit for that geographic area. The FDIC has set appraisal caps as follows:

Single Family	$101,250
Duplex	$114,000
Triplex	$138,000
Fourplex	$160,000

Eligible properties are made available under the Affordable Housing Program for 180 days. If they don't sell during that time, they may then be put on the open market and be sold to anyone, not just low and moderate-income buyers. However, FDIC subsidies and discounts still apply after the 180-day period for qualified buyers. See the next section for details.

Do You Qualify?

The FDIC's Affordable Housing Program defines a qualified buyer as a household with an adjusted income less than 115% of the median income for the area, taking the household size and location of the property into account. Median income represents the half-way point on the income scale in your area: half of the people make more than the median, and half the people make less. For more information on eligibility requirements, contact one of the Affordable Housing Coordinators on the following page.

Subsidies and Discounts

No matter how a property is financed—whether by a third party or by the FDIC itself—the FDIC's Affordable Housing Program will help with the closing costs, to the tune of 3% of the actual sales price or $1,500, whichever is greater.

Not only that, but for properties financed by a third party (your bank or other lender), the FDIC will provide you with an amount equal to 7% of the purchase price, which you can then use to pay the various costs of third party financing—among them, the actual costs of a loan application, credit reports, loan points, interest buydowns, principal buydowns, required escrows, mortgage title insurance premiums or endorsements, and appraisals.

The only restriction for Affordable Housing buyers is that you must agree to occupy the property you purchase for at least one year as your primary residence. If you relocate for employment reasons, this requirement can be waived. Usually, if a property is resold within one year, you must return 75% of any profit on the sale to the FDIC.

BUYER'S TIP:
Are you currently renting an FDIC property? If so, and if the property goes on the market, you can purchase it whether or not your are income qualified. Ask your FDIC Affordable Housing Coordinator for details.

Affordable Housing Coordinators

Northeast Service Center
(CT, VT, NH, NY, NJ, PA, PR, MA, RI, ME)
Affordable Housing Coordinator
101 E. River Dr.
Hartford, CT 06108
800-873-7785
E-mail: rneama@fdic.gov

Field Operations Branch
(for all Other States and the District of Columbia)
Affordable Housing Coordinator
1910 Pacific Ave.
Dallas, TX 75201
800-568-9161
E-mail: rolson@fdic.gov

Types of FDIC Sales

Some FDIC sales are handled by brokers, while others are handled directly by the FDIC sales staff. Open auctions and sealed bid auctions are also commonly used. Whatever the type of sale, all the terms and conditions for a particular property will be described by the sales contact person when you call.

To find out more about upcoming auctions, call the 800 number for the FDIC Affordable Housing Coordinator nearest you and press the option for "upcoming events" on the phone menu. Also, visit their web site: **www.fdic.gov/buying/owned.html**. Auctions and sealed bid announcements appear on their web site under "National Asset Sales Calendar - Real Estate Sales." These announcements will also appear in local and regional newspapers.

Many of properties are sold by sealed bid, which means you must write down your bid and submit it by a certain date. The FDIC accepts sealed bids by both mail and fax; the sales agent in charge of the property will provide you with complete instructions.

Investor Properties

A vast selection of larger commercial properties are available from the FDIC. These properties represent great investment opportunities for people with deep pockets.

The FDIC provides financing for properties in this classification when the sales price exceeds $500,000. Terms of financing and sale may be obtained from the person assigned to market the property. If you are interested in finding out more about these properties, contact the FDIC Affordable Housing Coordinators Service Center listed on the previous page.

10 REOs and Loans from the VA

The Veterans Administration (VA) is an excellent source of both loans and REO properties. And here's a little known fact: while you must have served in the military to be eligible for a traditional VA loan, *you do not have to be a veteran to buy or obtain financing on the VA's REO properties!*

You will find many VA properties included in the Foreclosed Property Listings that come with this catalog. To locate even more opportunities, you can call the VA's national 800 number for REO properties in your area: 1-800-827-1000. Ask for the Property Management Division. Another good idea is to contact your local VA office. For the address and phone number of the office nearest you, see Appendix B in this catalog.

The first section of this chapter will talk about REOs and the loans anyone can get on REO properties—even if you're not a veteran. The second part of this chapter will cover all the information you need on VA loans if you are in fact a veteran of the U.S. Armed Forces.

REOs Galore

VA offices in most states carry an impressive inventory of REOs. For example, in Oklahoma, around 75-125 properties are offered for sale every three weeks. Procedures for disposing of these properties vary from state to state. Some VA state offices will send you a list of VA-owned properties currently available in your area; other VA offices will only send their lists to real estate agents. VA property lists include the asking price and all the instructions for making an offer, which must be placed by sealed bid.

Ten days to two weeks before the closing bid date, the property for sale will be open for inspection. This is your chance to look it over and decide if you really want it. The VA makes no guarantees about the physical condition of the property—so by all means, play it safe and have an inspection done by a professional.

BUYER'S TIP:
Real estate brokers who advertise VA properties are not allowed to use the words "Foreclosure," "Repo," or "Repossessed" in their ads. Instead you will see the words, "Government-owned" or "Acquired," which mean the same thing.

All offers on VA-owned properties must go through real estate brokers. If the minimum bid on a property is not reached, it will be rolled over and offered again in the next selling period. If you are the highest bidder over the minimum price set by the VA, the property is yours!

Bargain Basement Prices

Prices on VA repos range from the ordinary to the ridiculous. In Oklahoma, single-family homes range from $100,000 to *just $500*, with the average price being $30,000 to $50,000 for a three-bedroom, one or one-and-a-half bath home with a two-car garage. All properties are sold "as is."

BUYER'S TIP:
In many states, the VA pays the real estate commission on any property you buy—yet another reason why VA repos are such great deals!

A very real advantage you get from buying a VA-owned property is that you can usually assume the existing VA loan! These loans often feature low interest rates, which means even more savings for you!

Loans for Everyone

We repeat: if you want to bid on a VA-owned property, you do NOT have to be a veteran either to buy it, or to qualify for a loan. There are two choices when it comes to loans: you can assume the existing loan on the property, pending the approval of the VA and your lender; and/or you can receive what is called a "term loan" from the VA to cover the balance, which offers mortgages of various lengths up to 30 years. You'll also be pleased to know that current VA interest rates are set at the low end of the spectrum.

BUYER'S TIP:
Earnest money deposits on VA REOs typically run about $500 for owner-occupants and $1,000 for investors. These amounts must be submitted with your sealed bid; for all unsuccessful bids, the money is returned.

The real estate broker in charge of the property will have the proper loan forms for you to fill out. If you place the winning bid, the broker will submit these forms along with the closing documents on the property.

And Now, Programs for All You Veterans

The VA does a good job of taking care of its own. For VA housing purposes, veterans include certain members of the Select Reserve, active duty service personnel, and some categories of spouses, as well as individuals who have completed their military service.

If you're a qualified veteran, join the crowd—since the end of World War II, over 14 million veterans have bought homes with VA loans! You must have served an appropriate length of time in any branch of the military to be eligible for what is called an entitlement to a loan. For veterans who began their service after 1980, this amount of time is usually two years. However, if you served at least 90 days in World War II, the Korean War, the Vietnam War, or the Persian Gulf conflict, you're in. Military personnel currently on active duty must have at least 180 days of service.

BUYER'S TIP:
For homes less than a year old that were not inspected by the VA or FHA during construction, the VA requires that the builder provide you with an insured 10-year protection plan, which protects you against defects in materials and workmanship. See VA Pamphlet 26-6 or ask your local VA office for details.

VA Guaranteed Loans

What the VA does for you, as a home-buying veteran, is guarantee part of your loan to improve your chances of qualifying. Here are the outstanding features of the VA loan program for veterans:

- No down payment is required! That's right, absolutely no down payment is necessary if you are a qualified veteran.
- Interest rates are extremely competitive, and you have the option of negotiating interest rates with your lender.
- There are no penalties for paying off the loan early. You can pay off all or part of your loan in advance without incurring penalties of any kind.

What the VA Guarantee is Not

The VA goes to great lengths to explain their guarantee. What the VA guarantees is ONLY your loan. Sometimes veterans assume that the VA also guarantees the condition of any house they buy, but this is not the case. The VA does not have the authority to guarantee that a house is free of defects, or that it is a good investment.

That's why it's so important to get a professional inspection done before you buy a home—especially a previously occupied home. Hire a qualified residential inspection service to do this for you. If defects are discovered, you then negotiate with the seller and the seller's real estate agent about what costs will be deducted from the purchase price.

For newly built homes, the VA usually requires a compliance inspection to see that the house meets accepted standards of good construction—and that it conforms to the plans on which the VA appraisal is based. If your new home is under construction, you can also file copies of the plans for your home with the VA, which will then do its best to see that the actual construction conforms to the plans.

Here's more good news: even though the VA does not guarantee the condition of any home, the agency may pay for correcting serious structural defects of a new home if they are discovered within four years of the time the loan is made. There are no forms to fill out; should this happen, you write a detailed letter to the Loan Guaranty Officer of the VA office nearest you. These situations are handled on a case-by-case basis.

BUYER'S TIP:
Interested in buying a mobile home? Call your local VA office listed in Appendix B of this book and ask for VA Pamphlet 26-71-1.

The VA Appraisal

Before you buy, the VA will appraise the house you want to determine its current market value. Your loan amount and terms of repayment will be based on this appraised value.

Equal Opportunity All the Way!

All eligible veterans have an equal opportunity to buy homes with VA assistance, without regard to race, color, religion, sex, handicap, family status, or national origin. All builders, brokers, and lenders must comply with this policy—it's the law!

If you suspect discrimination, your local VA office will investigate. Fill out and file VA Form 26-8827, Housing Discrimination Complaint, and let the VA take it from there.

Extra Help from Your VA Office

Are you looking for newly built homes available with VA financing? If you're having trouble finding these homes, your local VA office can help. See Appendix B for the office nearest you.

Another area where your local VA office can help is State housing programs. These programs are separate from Federal housing programs and requirements vary from state to state. Ask your VA office for information on programs you may qualify for in your state.

BUYER'S TIP:
There is a special VA Direct Home Loan program for Native American veterans living on trust lands. These loans can be used for building a home or for buying a home and making improvements on it. For more information, ask your local VA office for Pamphlet 26-93-1.

Certificate of Eligibility

To qualify for a VA loan, you must obtain a Certificate of Eligibility from your local VA office. To expedite your request, you will be required to complete the following:

- Fill out Form 26-1880, Request for Determination of Eligibility and Available Loan Guaranty Entitlement. Include your social security number and service number.
- Include an acceptable original Statement of Service or a copy of Member 4 of DD-214.
- List any past VA loans you have received on your application.
- If you received any VA loans in the past, include a copy of the Release of Mortgage or a letter from your lender on letterhead with an original signature, stating that you paid off the loan in full.
- Fill out Form #7C, which is a request for a duplicate Certificate of Eligibility.

Signing the Agreement

There's an important item to include when it comes time to sign the sales agreement for your new home: make sure the contract has a clause that provides for any cash deposit you make to be refunded if your VA loan does not come through. Occasionally veterans lose their deposits, and there's not much the VA can do to help you once that happens.

Assuming VA Loans

If you decide to sell your home and you have a VA loan made on or after March 1, 1988, another person cannot take over your loan payments unless they are approved by the VA or your lender.

If your VA loan was taken out before that date and you're not required to obtain approval for a new owner to assume it, you may still be liable for any claims paid in the event the new owner defaults—unless you obtain a release of liability from your lender and the VA. Obviously, it's to your advantage to obtain these releases, and we strongly recommend that you do so!

What about buying your next home? In order to reuse your VA loan entitlement, your VA loan must be paid in full at the time you sell your home—or you must sell to another vet who can substitute his or her entitlement for yours.

11 Other Bargain Property Sources

So far in this catalog, we've covered some of the nation's most popular sources for REO properties. We've talked about FDIC, VA, and HUD homes. We've also given you the inside scoop on the nation's two largest sources of home loans, Fannie Mae and Freddie Mac.

Now, in this chapter, we'll give you information on FIVE additional government agencies that sell bargain homes, farms, land, and investment properties. They are: the Internal Revenue Service (IRS); General Services Administration (GSA); Small Business Administration (SBA); State Surplus offices; and Rural Economic and Community Development Services (RECDS).

So read on to take advantage of even more opportunities for real estate bargains!

Internal Revenue Service (IRS)

IRS property sales represent truly amazing deals. Recently a house worth over $100,000 was set to go on the IRS auction block for a minimum bid of $17,000. How is that possible, you may ask?

In this example, the owners owed $17,000 in back taxes. All the IRS wants to do is recover the back tax amount. So unlike some government agencies that have to sell their properties at fair market value, the IRS is mainly interested in just getting their money out. They may not advertise this fact, but it's true!

All kinds of properties are offered for sale by the IRS. In Georgia recently, IRS-seized properties included a four-bedroom house on 1.7 acres with a separate garage, and a red

brick, two-story condo with three bedrooms and two baths. The minimum bids on these properties were just a fraction of their market value!

How IRS Property Sales Work

All IRS property sales are handled by the individual Revenue officer who seized the property. Some IRS offices have auction hotline numbers that give the specifics of properties currently for sale, as well as the phone numbers of the revenue offices handling the sales. The other offices advertise in the local paper(s). These revenue officers can answer any questions you may have. See Appendix D in this catalog for a list of IRS offices around the country.

Generally, IRS property sales are advertised in local newspapers. They may also post notices in the County Courthouse. In some states, like Georgia, bidding for IRS-seized properties sometimes takes place on the County Courthouse steps!

Most IRS offices do not keep sales lists, nor do they mail out information packets or brochures about their properties. The best way to find out about these deals is to read your local newspaper, and call your local IRS hotline periodically to see what's available.

BUYER'S TIP:
The U.S. Real Property Sales List contains a form you can fill out to receive listings of individual GSA properties for sale. You can specify exactly what type of property you're looking for, how much you want to pay and what state(s) you're interested in. Order this booklet today by calling 1-800-472-1313.

Financing for IRS-Seized Properties

IRS-seized properties are sold at auction to the highest bidder. When you find a property you want to bid on, you must go to your local lender and arrange your own financing. It helps if you've already been approved for a loan. (See Chapter 5, How to Get a Loan, for details.)

Usually you'll be asked to put up a percentage of the purchase price at bidding time as a down payment. For this purpose, cashier's checks are preferred. Depending on what part of the country you're in, the balance will be due either within 30 days or by the end of the auction day itself.

Most IRS auctions are held on weekdays, which is good because the banks are open. Some people bring their bankers with them to the auction, while others just go down to the bank after the bidding is over to pick up a cashier's check for the balance, if the balance is due on auction day.

General Services Administration (GSA)

The GSA sells most of the Federal government's surplus real estate. A good place to start is their national 800 number, 1-800-472-1313. When you call this number you can request a booklet called the *U.S. Real Property Sales List*, which contains information about the GSA and a list of properties that are currently for sale.

The GSA sells properties in all 50 states, the District of Columbia, Puerto Rico, the Virgin Islands, and the U.S. Pacific territories. Offerings range from military housing complexes and former Federal office buildings to individual family homes. The larger GSA properties are sold at auction, and the smaller properties (including homes) are usually sold by sealed bid.

GSA Bidding Procedures

When you find a property you want to bid on, the GSA requires you to put down a bid deposit. For sealed bids, you must obtain a special bidding form from your regional GSA office (see the list of GSA offices at the end of this section).

Sealed bids must be filed by a specific date. When they are opened, the property goes to the highest bidder at or above the minimum established by the GSA. Remember, most residential properties are sold by sealed bid, so be sure to follow these procedures to maximize your chances for success!

GSA Website

The website for GSA is useful in helping you find property you might be interested in. Type in this address on your internet browser, **http://propertydisposal.gsa.gov/property/**. This handy property disposal site has a map where you can click on images of the state or states where you'd like to purchase property. You will then get photos of the property, address, description and an e-mail link to the point of contact person.

You can get additional information about GSA at their main website, **http://www.gsa.gov**.

GSA Regional Offices

The GSA has four regional sales offices and two field offices. Write or call these offices for more information about specific properties or about the sales program in general.

REGIONAL OFFICES

Boston Real Estate Sales Office
617-565-5700
Mailing Address:
U.S. General Services Administration
Property Disposal Division
10 Causeway St., Room 1079
Boston, MA 02222
States Covered: Massachusetts, Maine, New Hampshire, Vermont, Rhode Island, Connecticut, New Jersey, New York, Ohio, Michigan, Indiana, Illinois, Wisconsin, Minnesota, Puerto Rico, Virgin Islands

Atlanta Real Estate Sales Office
404-331-5133
Mailing Address:
U.S. General Services Administration
Property Disposal Division
401 W. Peachtree St., Suite 2928
Atlanta, GA 30365-2550
States Covered: Georgia, Florida, Mississippi, Alabama, South Carolina, North Carolina, Tennessee, Kentucky, Virginia, West Virginia, Pennsylvania, Delaware, Maryland, District of Columbia

Fort Worth Real Estate Sales Office
800-833-4317
Mailing Address:
U.S. General Services Administration
Property Disposal Division
819 Taylor St.
Fort Worth, TX 76102
States Covered: Texas, Louisiana, Arkansas, Missouri, Iowa, Oklahoma, Kansas, Nebraska, South Dakota, North Dakota, Montana, Wyoming, Utah, Colorado, New Mexico

BUYER'S TIP:
The GSA sells all kinds of government surplus items, from cars and trucks to furniture, computers, tools, and more! For details, consult the *National Auction Catalog*, another great publication available from Bargain Property Network. Call 1-800-522-2730 to order today! Ask the operator for extension 1000.

San Francisco Real Estate Sales Office
800-421-7848
253-931-7962-Hotline
Mailing Address:
U.S. General Services Administration
Property Disposal Division
450 Golden Gate Ave.
San Francisco, CA 94102
States Covered: California, Arizona, Nevada, Idaho, Oregon, Washington, Alaska, Hawaii, Guam

FIELD OFFICES

Office of Real Estate Sales
U.S. General Services Administration
230 South Dearborn St., Room 3756
Chicago, IL 60604
312-353-6045

Office of Real Estate Sales
U.S. General Services Administration
400 15th St. SW, Room 1138
Auburn, WA 98001-6599
253-931-7547

Small Business Administration (SBA)

The SBA is a little-known source of real estate bargains. At any one time, the SBA has between 450-500 REO properties available nationwide. These include both residential and commercial properties—everything from manufacturing concerns to franchises and all kinds of businesses.

While the focus of the SBA is on commercial properties, you can definitely pick up good deals on residential real estate as well. SBA properties are sold at auction, and cash is the preferred method of payment. However, terms can be arranged, especially when the property is being handled by a broker. Because the SBA handles so many different kinds of properties, payment terms are structured to suit each individual property and buyer.

Get on the Net

The quickest and easiest way to locate SBA properties nationwide is on the Information Superhighway. If you don't have a computer with access to the World Wide Web, find someone who does and look up the SBA at the following on-line address: http://www.financenet.gov

This computerized list allows you to access SBA properties by both location and type of property. The listings include minimum bids and the person to contact for more information.

You will also find government assets for sale at the above on-line address through a variety of other agencies, including HUD, U.S. Customs, GSA, and FDIC. So as you can see, the World Wide Web is like your own Home Shopping Channel for real estate deals from government agencies!

BUYER'S TIP:
The quickest way to find SBA properties is on the information superhighway. You'll find SBA listings at the following on-line address: http://www.financenet.gov

SBA Sales Procedures

When you find an SBA property that interests you, either via the World Wide Web or by calling the SBA offices directly (See Appendix F in this catalog for listings), you must contact the SBA officer who is handling that sale for particulars. SBA properties are first offered at public auctions conducted by a professional auction house.

If the minimum auction bid is not met, the SBA will use other means to dispose of the property, including listings with residential or commercial real estate brokers—and that's when the deals really get good! So keep your eyes on the newspaper as well, since SBA properties handled by brokers will often be advertised locally.

United States Marshals Service (USMS)

Through forfeiture by government agencies enforcing the law, the United States Marshals Service offers both real estate property and personal property for sale to the public. The types of real estate available are residential, commercial and business establishments. Usually this property is sold by local real estate brokers with multiple listing services. Less frequently, properties are sold through GSA or USMS directly.

USMS does not provide a list of forfeited properties for sale. You can, however, find additional useful information on their website: **www.usdov.gov/marshals**.

Their personal property sales are usually done by auction. You can find boats, aircrafts, vehicles, jewelry, art, antiques and collectibles. USMS has a National Sellers List (NSL) with USMS contractors and government agencies who auction these forfeited items. Access the NSL through their website: **www.usdov.gov/marshals** or **www.pueblo.gsa.gov**. You can also get the list by a fax on demand service: (202) 307-9777. Finally, you can order a copy through the mail by sending a check or money order for 50¢ to: Consumer Information Center, Dept. 386E, Pueblo, CO 81009.

State Surplus Agencies

State Surplus offices are best known for selling used government vehicles and office equipment to the public. However, in some states you'll find real estate offered as well.

Call your State Surplus office (See Appendix E for listings) and ask for the real estate division. You'll either be told that they don't handle real estate, or you'll be given a direct line for real estate sales.

State Surplus properties tend to be rare, but when they come up they can be very unusual and very good deals. For example, in North Carolina, the state sells real estate at public auction a couple of times a year. Offerings include tracts of land that the state no longer needs—for example, a remote forest cabin with a lookout tower. Sales are advertised in the local papers and anyone is allowed to place a bid.

Procedures vary from state to state, but generally speaking, your best bet is to stay in phone contact with your State Surplus agency and see what comes up. It's like fishing—you may wait a long time, and then come up with a big one, like that cabin in the woods. The deals are out there—you just need a bit of patience and persistence to find them.

BUYER'S TIP:
To qualify for Alaska's Homestead program, you must meet certain basic requirements: you must be a U.S. citizen at least 18 years of age; and you must be an Alaskan resident for at least one year immediately prior to applying.

What About Homesteading?

By and large, homesteading programs have been disbanded nationwide. It used to be that you could take part in HUD's Urban Homesteading Program in 23 cities nationwide, where you could pick up REOs for as little as $1 a piece! But even though most homesteading opportunities have bitten the dust, there is one important exception: Alaska.

Yes, homesteading is alive and well in Alaska, the last frontier! Call the Alaska Department of Natural Resources at 907-269-8400 and ask for a brochure on their Homestead Programs.

Homesteads are larger parcels, up to 160 acres, in more remote areas. The way you qualify for this program is by "proving up," which means you can acquire state-owned land by doing three things:

- Building a habitable, permanent dwelling.
- Living on the land for a certain period of time.
- Paying some of the costs involved, such as surveying.

What Kinds of Properties Are Available?

Alaskan homestead properties are usually in remote locations which may not be accessible by roads. For now, you get there by plane, boat, rail, snowmobile, dog sled,

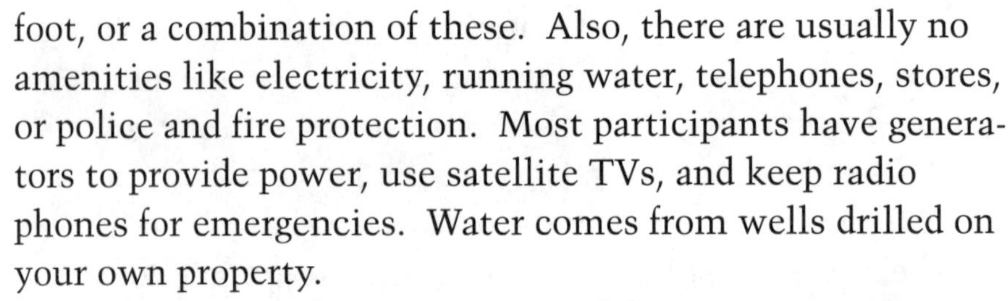

foot, or a combination of these. Also, there are usually no amenities like electricity, running water, telephones, stores, or police and fire protection. Most participants have generators to provide power, use satellite TVs, and keep radio phones for emergencies. Water comes from wells drilled on your own property.

BUYER'S TIP:
When you call your local RECDS office, ask to be put on the mailing list in your area. If farm and rural properties interest you, you'll be glad you did.

Alaskan real estate is some of the most magnificent in the world. If you have a sense of adventure and the urge to relocate, this could be the perfect opportunity for you!

Rural Economic and Community Development Services (RECDS)

This agency used to be known as the Farmers Home Administration, or FmHA. There's been a great deal of reorganization happening within this government sector, but the bottom line is that there are plenty of farm and rural properties available—plus money for both farm and nonfarm loans!

Here's what to do: consult your local telephone directory for the number of the RECDS County Office nearest you. Your local RECDS office can provide you with a complete list of properties currently available in your area, plus applications for the various RECDS loan programs, which include: farm operating and ownership loans, rural housing loans, self-help housing loans, home improvement loans—even rental housing loans!

To qualify for RECDS loans, you must be unable to obtain enough loan money elsewhere at reasonable rates and terms. This is because the RECDS is a supplemental lender and is not in competition with other commercial lenders.

The RECDS offers a wide variety of farm properties in a wide variety of price ranges, including some of the most affordable rural and farm properties you'll find anywhere. And all it takes is a phone call to get started on your quest for real estate bargains today!

Appendix A
HUD Offices

Information on HUD is also available via their website:

www.hud.gov/local.html

"HUD next door kiosk" indicates the location of an interactive computer (similar to an ATM machine) that will assist you in locating properties.

ALABAMA STATE OFFICE

Birmingham
U.S. Dept. of Housing and Urban Development
600 Beacon Parkway West
Suite 300
Birmingham, AL 35209
205-290-7630
Fax: 205-290-7593
TTY: 205-290-7624

ALASKA STATE OFFICE

Anchorage
VECO Alaska Building
949 East 36th Ave., Suite 401
Anchorage, AK 99508-4399
907-271-4663
Fax: 907-271-3667
TTY: 907-271-4328
HUD next door kiosk
Northway Mall
3101 Penland Park
Anchorage, AK 99508-1955

Michaelson, Connor & Boul, Inc. is a primary contractor to the Dept. of Housing and Urban Development providing marketing and management services of HUD owned residential 1 to 4 unit properties in Alaska, Ohio, Maryland, Michigan & West Virginia. Visit their website at: www.mcbreo.com

ARIZONA STATE OFFICES

Phoenix
400 N. 5th St., Suite 1600
Phoenix, AZ 85004
602-379-4461
Fax: 602-379-3985
TTY: 602-379-4464
HUD next door kiosk
Phoenix Public Library
1221 N. Central Ave.
Phoenix, AZ 85004

Tucson
33 N. Stone Ave., Suite 700
Tucson, AZ 85701
520-670-6000
Fax: 520-670-6207

ARKANSAS STATE OFFICE

Little Rock
425 W. Capitol, Suite 900
Little Rock, AR 72201
501-324-5931
Fax: 501-324-5900
TTY: 501-324-5931
HUD next door kiosk
Park Plaza Mall
6000 W. Markham St.
Little Rock, AR

CALIFORNIA STATE OFFICES

San Francisco
450 Golden Gate Ave.
San Francisco, CA 94102-3448
415-436-6550
Fax: 415-436-6510
HUD next door kiosk
on the lobby level of the Philip Burton Federal Building
450 Golden Gate Ave.
San Francisco, CA 94102-3448

Appendix A (cont.)
HUD Offices

Fresno
Crocker Building
2135 Fresno St., Suite 100
Fresno, CA 93721-1718
559-487-5033
Fax: 559-487-5344
HUD next door kiosk
Manchester Mall
1901 E. Shields Ave.
Fresno, CA 93726

Los Angeles
AT&T Building
611 W. Sixth St., Suite 800
Los Angeles, CA 90017
213-894-8000
Fax: 213-894-8096
TTY: 213-894-8133
HUD next door kiosk
Los Angeles Public Library
630 W. Fifth St.
Los Angeles, CA 90071

Sacramento
925 L St.
Sacramento, CA 95814
916-498-5220
Fax: 916-498-5262
TTY: 916-498-5959
HUD next door kiosk
Sacramento Storefront
925 L Street
Sacremento, CA 95814

San Diego
Mission City Corporate Center
2365 Northside Dr., Suite 300
San Diego, CA 92108-2712
Near Qualcomm Stadium
off Friars Rd.
619-557-5305
Fax: 619-557-6296
TTY: 619-557-2604
HUD next door kiosk
City Hall
202 C St.
San Diego, CA 92101

Santa Ana
1600 N. Broadway, Suite 100
Santa Ana, CA 92706-3927
888-827-5605
Fax: 714-796-1285

COLORADO STATE OFFICE

Denver
633 17th St.
Denver, CO 80202
303-672-5440
Fax: 303-672-5004
TTY: 303-672-5248

CONNECTICUT STATE OFFICE

Hartford
One Corporate Center
19th Floor
Hartford, CT 06103-3220
860-240-4800 - Hotline
HUD next door kiosk
New Haven City Hall
165 Church St.
New Haven, CT 06510

DELAWARE STATE OFFICE

Wilmington
824 Market St., Suite 850
Wilmington DE 19801-3016
302-573-6300
Fax: 302-573-6259
TTD: 302-573-6058
HUD next door kiosk
Delaware HSS
North East Service Center
1624 Jessip St.
Wilmington, DE 19802
www.firstpreston.com

Appendix A (cont.)
HUD Offices

FLORIDA STATE OFFICES

Miami
Brickell Plaza Federal Building
909 SE First Ave., Rm. 500
Miami, FL 33131-3028
305-536-4456
Fax: 305-536-4698
HUD next door kiosk
S.P. Clark Government Center
111 N.W. 1st St.
Miami, FL 33128

Jacksonville
301 W. Bay St., Suite 2200
Jacksonville, FL 32202
904-232-2627
Fax: 904-232-3759
TTY: 904-232-2631
HUD next door kiosk
Jacksonville Public Library
122 North Ocean St.
Jacksonville, FL 32202

Orlando
3751 Maguire Blvd., Suite 270
Orlando, FL 32803
407-648-6441
Fax: 407-648-6310
HUD next door kiosk
Orlando Public Library
101 E. Central Blvd.
Orlando, FL 32801

Tampa
Timberlake Federal
Office Building
500 Zack St., Suite 402
Tampa, FL 33602-3945
813-228-2026
813-228-2504 - Hotline
Fax: 813-228-2431
TTY: 813-228-2115
HUD next door kiosk
Seminole Heights Branch
Tampa/Hillsborough County
Public Library
4711 Central Ave.
Tampa, FL 33603

GEORGIA STATE OFFICE

Atlanta
Five Points Plaza Building
40 Marietta St.
Atlanta, GA 30303
404-331-5136
Fax: 404-730-2149
TTY: 404-730-2654
HUD next door kiosk
Atlanta Storefront
Five Points Plaza
40 Marietta St.
Atlanta, GA 30303-2806
HUD next door kiosk
Atlanta City Hall East
675 Ponce DeLeon Ave.
Atlantic, GA 30308

HAWAII STATE OFFICE

Honolulu
Seven Waterfront Plaza, Ste. 500
500 Ala Moana Blvd.
Honolulu, HI 96813
808-522-8185
Fax: 808-522-8194
Fax: 808-522-8170
TTY: 808-522-8193

IDAHO STATE OFFICE

Boise
Plaza IV, Suite 220
800 Park Blvd.
Boise, ID 83712
208-334-1990 - Hotline
Fax: 208-334-9648
TTY: 208-334-9094
HUD next door kiosk
Boise Towne Square Mall
350 N. Milwaukee
Boise, ID 83788

Appendix A (cont.)
HUD Offices

ILLINOIS STATE OFFICE

Chicago
Ralph H. Metcalfe Federal Bldg.
77 W. Jackson Blvd.
Chicago, IL 60604
312-353-5680
Fax: 312-886-2729
TTY: 312-261-5944
HUD next door kiosk
Healthy East Chicago, Inc.
100 W. Chicago Ave.
East Chicago, IN 46312
HUD next door kiosk
Ralph Metcalfe Federal Building
77 W. Jackson Blvd.
Chicago, IL 60604-3507

INDIANA STATE OFFICE

Indianapolis
151 N. Delaware St.
Indianapolis, IN 46204-2526
317-226-6303
Homes for sale are contracted out to Golden Feather, Reality Inc:
888-660-9911
HUD next door kiosk
City Hall
200 E. Market St.
Indianapolis, IN 46204

IOWA STATE OFFICE

Des Moines
210 Walnut, Rm. 239
Des Moines, IA 50309-2155
515-284-4512
Fax: 515-284-4743
HUD next door kiosk
Des Moines Federal Building
210 Walnut St.
Des Moines, IA 50303-4514

KANSAS STATE OFFICE

Kansas City
400 State Ave., Gateway Tower II
Kansas City, KS 66101
913-551-5644
Fax: 913-551-5416
Homes for sale are contracted out to First Preston:
800-487-3808
www.firstpreston.com
HUD next door kiosk
Indian Springs Mall
4601 State Ave.
Kansas City, KS

KENTUCKY STATE OFFICE

Louisville
U.S. Deptartment of HUD
Gene Snyder Courthouse
601 W. Broadway
Louisville, KY 40202
502-582-5251
Fax: 502-828-6074
HUD next door kiosk
Louisville Urban League
1535 W. Broadway
Louisville, KY

LOUISIANA STATE OFFICES

New Orleans
Hale Boggs Federal Bldg.
Ninth Floor
501 Magazine St.
New Orleans, LA 70130-3099
504-589-7201
Fax: 504-589-6619
TTY: 504-589-7277
HUD next door kiosk
City Hall
1300 Perdido St.
New Orleans, LA 70112

Appendix A (cont.)
HUD Offices

Shreveport
401 Edwards St., Suite 1510
Shreveport, LA 71101-5513
318-676-3385
Fax Single Family: 318-676-3408
Fax Multifamily: 308-676-3432
Fax Administration: 318-676-6407
TTY: 318-676-3399
HUD next door kiosk
City of Shreveport, Louisiana
1237 Murphy St.
Shreveport, LA 71101

MAINE STATE OFFICE

Bangor
Margaret Chase Smith
Federal Building
202 Harlow St., Rm. 101
Bangor, ME 04401
Mailing Address:
P.O. Box 1384
Bangor, ME 04402-1384
207-945-0467
Fax: 207-945-0533
TTY: 207-945-0469

MARYLAND STATE OFFICE

Baltimore
City Crescent Building
10 S. Howard St., Fifth Floor
Baltimore, MD 21201-2505
410-962-2520
Fax: 410-962-0668
TTY: 410-962-0106
HUD next door kiosk
Baltimore Storefront
City Crescent Building
10 S. Howard St., Suite 111
Baltimore, MD 21201
HUD next door kiosk
Prince Georges County
9400 Peppercorn Place
Largo, MD 21774

MASSACHUSETTS STATE OFFICE

Boston
Thomas P. O'Neill
Federal Building
10 Causeway St., Suite 375
Boston, MA 02222-1092
617-565-5234
Fax: 617-565-5257
TTY: 617-565-5168 Mon.– Fri.
HUD next door kiosk
Thomas O'Neill Federal Building
10 Causeway St.
Boston, MA 02222-1092

MICHIGAN STATE OFFICES

Detroit
Patrick V. McNamara
Federal Building
477 Michigan Ave., Suite 1700
Detroit, MI 48226
313-226-7900
Fax: 313-226-5611
TTY: 313-226-6899
HUD next door kiosk
Detroit City/County Building
1Woodward Ave.
Mail Level
Detroit, MI 48226

Michaelson, Connor & Boul, Inc.
is a primary contractor to the Dept. of Housing and Urban Development providing marketing and management services of HUD owned residential 1 to 4 unit properties in Alaska, Ohio, Maryland, Michigan & West Virginia. Visit their website at:
www.mcbreo.com

Appendix A (cont.)
HUD Offices

Flint
605 N. Saginaw St., Rm. 200
Flint, MI 48502
810-766-5110
Fax: 810-766-5122
TTY: 810-766-5106
HUD next door kiosk
Flint City Hall
1101 S. Saginaw
Flint, MI 48502

Grand Rapids
50 Louis NW
Grand Rapids, MI 49503-2648
616-456-2100
Fax: 616-456-2187
TTY: 616-456-2159

MINNESOTA STATE OFFICE

Minneapolis
Bridge Place Building
220 Second St. South
Minneapolis, MN 55401
612-370-3000
Fax: 612-370-3220
TTY: 612-370-3186
HUD next door kiosk
Public Service Center
250 S. 4th St.
Minneapolis, MN 55401

MISSISSIPPI STATE OFFICE

Jackson
Dr. A. H. McCoy Federal Building
100 W. Capitol St., Suite 910
Jackson, MS 39260-1096
601-965-4700
Fax: 601-965-4773

MISSOURI STATE OFFICE

St. Louis
Robert A. Young Federal
Office Building
1222 Spruce St., Rm. 3-207
St. Louis, MO 63103-2836
314-539-6583
Fax: 314-539-6384
TTY: 314-539-6331
HUD next door kiosk
Northwest Plaza Shopping Ctr.
650 Northwest Plaza
St. Ann, MO 63074

MONTANA STATE OFFICE

Helena
Power Block Building
7 West 6th Ave.
Helena, MT 59601
406-449-5050
Fax: 406-449-5052

NEBRASKA STATE OFFICE

Omaha
10909 Mill Valley Rd.
Suite 100
Omaha, NE 68154
402-492-3100
Fax: 402-492-3150
TTY: 402-492-3183
HUD next door kiosk
Crossroads Mall
72nd and Dodge Ave.
Omaha, NE 68114

Appendix A (cont.)
HUD Offices

NEVADA STATE OFFICES

Las Vegas
333 N. Rancho Rd., Suite 700
Las Vegas, NV 89106
702-388-6500
Fax: 702-388-6207
HUD next door kiosk
Las Vegas City Hall
400 E. Stewart
Las Vegas, NV 89101

Reno Storefront
Sierra Marketplace
3702 S. Virginia St., Suite G2
Reno, NV 89502
775-784-5383
Fax: 775-784-5066
HUD next door kiosk
City Hall
490 S. Center St.
Reno, NV 89505
HUD next door kiosk
Reno Storefront
3702 S. Virginia St.
Reno, NV 89502

NEW HAMPSHIRE STATE OFFICE

Manchester
Norris Cotton Federal Office Building
275 Chestnut St., 5th Floor
Manchester, NH 03101-2487
603-666-7510 x3901
603-666-7441
Fax: 603-666-7736
TTY: 603-666-7529
HUD next door kiosk
Norris Cotton Federal Building
275 Chestnut St.
Manchester, NH 03101

NEW JERSEY STATE OFFICES

Newark
One Newark Center, 13th Floor
1085 Raymond Blvd.
Newark, NJ 07102-5260
973-622-7900
Fax: 973-645-6239
TTY: 973-645-3298
HUD next door kiosk
Peter Podino Federal Building
970 Broad St.
Newark, NJ 02102
Homes for sale are contracted out to First Preston:
800-487-3045
www.firstpreston.com

Camden
Hudson Building
800 Hudson Square, 2nd Floor
Camden, NJ 08102-1156
609-757-5081
Fax: 609-757-5373
Homes for sale are contracted out to First Preston:
800-487-3045
www.firstpreston.com

NEW MEXICO STATE OFFICE

Albuquerque
625 Silver Ave., SW, Suite 100
Albuquerque, NM 87102-3185
505-346-6463
Fax: 505-346-6604
TTY: 800-877-8339
HUD next door kiosk
Albuquerque Storefront
625 Silver Ave., SW
Albuquerque, NM 87102

Appendix A (cont.)
HUD Offices

NEW YORK STATE OFFICES

New York City
Jacob K. Javits Federal Building
26 Federal Plaza, Rm. 3541
New York, NY 10278-0068
212-264-6500
Fax: 212-264-0246
TTY: 212-264-0927
HUD next door kiosk
Jacob Javits Federal Building
26 Federal Plaza
New York, NY 10278-0068
Homes for sale are contracted out to First Preston:
800-487-3045
www.firstpreston.com

Albany
52 Corporate Circle
Albany, NY 12203
518-464-4200
Fax: 518-464-4300
HUD next door kiosk
Albany Public Library
161 Washington Ave.
Albany, NY 12210
Homes for sale are contracted out to First Preston:
800-487-3045
www.firstpreston.com

Buffalo
Lafayette Court, 5th Floor
465 Main St.
Buffalo, NY 14203-1780
716-551-5755
Fax: 716-551-5752
TTY: 716-551-5787
HUD next door kiosk
Buffalo Storefront
465 Main St.
Lafayette Court
Buffalo, NY 14203
Homes for sale are contracted out to First Preston:
800-487-3045
www.firstpreston.com

NORTH CAROLINA STATE OFFICE

Greensboro
Koger Building
2306 W. Meadowview Rd.
Greensboro, NC 27407-3707
336-547-4000
Fax: 336-547-4015

NORTH DAKOTA STATE OFFICE

Fargo
657 2nd Ave. North
P.O. Box 2483
Fargo, ND 58108-2483
701-239-5040
Fax: 701-239-5249
TTY: 701-239-5668

OHIO STATE OFFICES

Columbus
Federal Office Building
200 N. High St., 7th Floor
Columbus, OH 43215
614-469-5737
Fax: 614-469-2432
TTY: 614-469-6694
HUD next door kiosk
Bricker Federal Building
200 North High St.
Columbus, OH 43215-2499

Michaelson, Connor & Boul, Inc.
is a primary contractor to the Dept. of Housing and Urban Development providing marketing and management services of HUD owned residential 1 to 4 unit properties in Alaska, Ohio, Maryland, Michigan & West Virginia. Visit their website at: www.mcbreo.com

Appendix A (cont.)
HUD Offices

Cincinnati
15 E. Seventh St., First Floor
Cincinnati, OH 45202-3188
513-684-3451
Fax: 513-684-6224
TTY: 513-684-6180

Cleveland
1350 Euclid Ave., Suite 500
Cleveland, OH 44115-1815
216-522-4058
Fax: 216-522-4067
TTY: 216-522-2261
HUD next door kiosk
Cleveland City Hall
601 Lakeside Ave., NE
Cleveland, OH 44114

OKLAHOMA STATE OFFICES

Oklahoma City
500 West Main, 4th Floor
Suite 400
Oklahoma City, OK 73102
405-553-7500
Fax: 405-553-7588
TTY: 405-553-7480
HUD next door kiosk
Walmart Super Center
6100 W. Reno
Oklahoma City, OK 73127

Tulsa
1516 S. Boston Ave., Suite 100
Tulsa, OK 74119
918-581-7168
800-594-9057
Fax: 918-581-7722
HUD next door kiosk
Tulsa Community College
3727 E. Apache
Tulsa, OK 74115

OREGON STATE OFFICE

Portland
400 SW 6th Ave., Suite 700
Portland, OR 97204
503-326-2561
Fax: 503-326-2568
Fax: 503-326-3097
HUD next door kiosk
Northeast Urban League
One Stop Career Center
3034 NE MLD Blvd.
Portland, OR 97212

PENNSYLVANIA STATE OFFICES

Philadelphia
This office also services Delaware.

The Wanamaker Building
100 Penn Square East
Philadelphia, PA 19107-3380
215-656-0600
Fax: 215-656-3433
TTY: 215-656-3452
HUD next door kiosk
9th and Market Streets
Philadelphia, PA 19107-9998
Homes for sale are contracted out to First Preston:
800-487-3045
www.firstpreston.com

Appendix A (cont.)
HUD Offices

Pittsburgh
339 Sixth Ave., 6th Floor
Pittsburgh, PA 15222-2515
412-644-6428
Fax: 412-644-6499
Fax Contact: 412-644-5857
TTY: 412-644-5747
HUD next door kiosk
200 Ross St.
Pittsburgh, PA 15222
Homes for sale are contracted out to First Preston:
800-487-3045
www.firstpreston.com

RHODE ISLAND STATE OFFICE

Providence
10 Weybosset St.
Providence, RI 02903
401-528-5351

SOUTH CAROLINA STATE OFFICE

Columbia
Strom Thurmond Federal Building
1835 Assembly St., 11th Floor
Columbia, SC 29201
HUD next door kiosk
1835 Assembly St.
Columbia, SC 29201-2480

SOUTH DAKOTA STATE OFFICE

Sioux Falls
2400 W. 49th St.
Suite I-201
Sioux Falls, SD 57105-6558
605-330-4223
Fax: 605-330-4465
TTY: 605-330-4223
HUD next door kiosk
Soiux Falls Public Library
201 N. Main Ave.
Sioux Falls, SD 57105

TENNESSEE STATE OFFICES

Nashville
251 Cumberland Bend
Suite 200
Nashville, TN 37228-1803
HUD next door kiosk
Kroger Superstore
3930 Clarksville Pike
Nashville, TN

Knoxville
John J. Duncan Federal Building
710 Locust St., S.W.
Knoxville, TN 37902-2526
423-545-4384
Fax: 423-545-4569
TTY: 423-545-4559
HUD next door kiosk
Knoxville County Clerk Office
Knoxville Center
3045 A Mall Road
Knoxville, TN 37924

Memphis
200 Jefferson, Suite 1200
Memphis, TN 38103
901-544-3367
Fax: 901-544-3697
TTY: 901-544-3053
HUD next door kiosk
Memphis, LG & W Div.
North Community Bus Office
2424 Summer Ave.
Memphis, TN

Appendix A (cont.)
HUD Offices

TEXAS STATE OFFICES

Fort Worth
Burnett Plaza Building
801 Cherry St.
Fort Worth, TX 76102
817-978-5965
Fax: 817-978-5567
TTD: 817-978-5596
HUD next door kiosk
City Hall Annex
Fort Worth Water Department
908 Monroe St.
Fort Worth, TX 76101

Dallas
A. Maceo Smith
Federal Office Building
525 Griffin St., Suite 860
Dallas, TX 75502-5007
214-767-8300
Fax: 214-767-8973
TTY: 214-767-4140
HUD next door kiosk
Southwest Center Mall
3662 W. Camp Wisdom Rd.
Dallas, TX 75237

Houston
2211 Norfolk, Suite 2000
Houston, TX 77098
713-313-2274 x7001
Fax: 713-313-2371
HUD next door kiosk
City Hall Annex
900 Bagby Rd.
Houston, TX 77002

Lubbock
George H. Mahon
Federal Office Building
1205 Texas Ave., Suite 511
Lubbock, TX 79401
806-472-7265
Fax: 806-472-7275
TTY: 800-887-8339
HUD next door kiosk
Mahon Public Library
1306 9th St.
Lubbock, TX 79401

San Antonio
Washington Square Building
800 Dolorosa
San Antonio, TX 78207
210-475-6806
Fax: 210-472-6804
TTY: 210-475-6885
HUD next door kiosk
South Park Mall
2310 S.W. Military Dr.
Suite 136
San Antonio, TX 78224

UTAH STATE OFFICE

Salt Lake City
257 East 200 South, Suite 550
Salt Lake City, UT 84111-2048
801-524-6070
Fax: 801-524-3439
TTY: 801-524-6909
HUD next door kiosk
Harmon's Grocery Store
3955 W. 3500 South
Salt Lake City, UT 84120
HUD next door kiosk
Harmon's Grocery Store
37 Harrisville Rd.
Ogden, UT 84404

Appendix A (cont.)
HUD Offices

VERMONT STATE OFFICE

Burlington
U.S. Federal Building, Rm. 237
11 Elmwood Ave.
P.O. Box 879
Burlington, VT 05402-0879
802-951-6290
Fax: 802-951-6298
HUD next door kiosk
Rental Opportunity Center
57 N. Champlain St.
Burlington, VT 05401

VIRGINIA STATE OFFICE

Richmond
3600 Center
3600 West Broad St.
Richmond, VA 23230-4920
804-278-4500
800-842-2610
Fax: 804-278-4603
TTY: 804-278-4501
HUD next door kiosk
Richmond Public Library
101 E. Franklin St.
Richmond, VA 23219

WASHINGTON STATE OFFICES

Seattle
Seattle Federal Office Building
909 1st Ave., Suite 200
Seattle, WA 98104-1000
206-220-5104
HUD next door kiosk
Jackson Federal Building
914 Second Ave.
Seattle, WA 98104-1000

Spokane
U.S. Courthouse Building
920 W. Riverside, Suite 588
Spokane, WA 99201
509-353-0674
HUD next door kiosk
Spokane Transit Authority Plaza Bldg.
2nd Floor Skywalk Level
701 W. Riverside Ave.
Spokane, WA

WASHINGTON, D.C. FIELD OFFICE

Metropolitan DC
820 First St., NE, Suite 300
Washington, DC 20002
202-275-9200
Fax: 202-523-4399
TTY: 202-275-0967
Storefront Office
801 N. Capitol St.
NE Washington, DC 20002
202-275-9200
Fax: 202-523-4399
TTY: 202-275-0967

Appendix A (cont.)
HUD Offices

WEST VIRGINIA STATE OFFICE

Charleston
405 Capitol St., Suite 708
Charleston, WV 25301-1795
304-347-7000
Fax: 304-347-7050
TTY: 304-347-5332
HUD next door kiosk
Kroger's, McCorkle Ave.
Charlston, WV
Michaelson, Connor & Boul, Inc.
is a primary contractor to the Dept. of Housing and Urban Development providing marketing and management services of HUD owned residential 1 to 4 unit properties in Alaska, Ohio, Maryland, Michigan & West Virginia. Visit their website at: www.mcbreo.com

WISCONSIN STATE OFFICE

Milwaukee
Henry Reuss Federal Plaza
310 W. Wisconsin Ave.
Milwaukee, WI 53203-2289
414-297-3214
Fax: 414-297-3947
TTY: 414-297-1423
HUD next door kiosk
310 W. Wisconsin Ave.
Milwaukee, WI 53203-2289

WYOMING STATE OFFICE

Casper
Federal Office Building
100 E. B St., Rm. 4229
Casper, WY 82601-1918
307-261-6250
Fax: 307-261-6245
TTY: 307-261-6258
HUD next door kiosk
Casper Storefront
150 East B St.
Casper, WY 82601

Appendix B
VA Offices

LOAN GUARANTY SERVICE
REGIONAL OFFICE ADDRESS LIST

NEW HAMPSHIRE OFFICE
Jurisdiction: Connecticut, Massachusetts, Maine, New Hampshire, Vermont

Department of Veterans Affairs
VA Regional Loan Center
275 Chestnut St.
Manchester, NH 03101
603-666-7502

OHIO OFFICE
Jurisdiction: Indiana, Michigan, New Jersey, Ohio, Pennsylvania

Department of Veterans Affairs
Cleveland Regional Loan Center
1240 East Ninth St.
Cleveland, OH 44199
800-729-5772

VIRGINIA OFFICE
Jurisdiction: District of Columbia, Kentucky, Maryland, Virginia, West Virginia

Department of Veterans Affairs
Roanoke Regional Loan Center
210 Franklin Rd. SW
Roanoke, VA 24011
800-933-5499

GEORGIA OFFICE
Jurisdiction: Georgia, North Carolina, South Carolina, Tennessee

Department of Veterans Affairs
VA Regional Loan Center
730 Peachtree St. NE
Atlanta, GA 30365
888-768-2132

FLORIDA OFFICE
Jurisdiction: Alabama, Florida, Mississippi

Department of Veterans Affairs
VA Regional Loan Center
P.O. Box 1437
St. Petersburg, FL 33731-1437
Outside FL: 888-611-5916
Within FL: 800-827-1000

MINNESOTA OFFICE
Jurisdiction: Illinois, Iowa, Kansas, Minnesota, Missouri, Nebraska, Wisconsin

Department of Veterans Affairs
VA Regional Loan Center
Fort Snelling
1 Federal Dr.
St. Paul, MN 55111-4050
800-827-0611

Appendix B (cont.)
VA Offices

TEXAS OFFICE
Jurisdiction: Arkansas, Kentucky, Louisiana, Mississippi, Oklahoma, Texas

Department of Veterans Affairs
VA Regional Loan Center
6900 Almeda Rd.
Houston, TX 77030
888-232-2571

COLORADO OFFICE
Jurisdiction: Alaska, Colorado, Idaho, Montana, New Mexico, Oregon, Washington

Department of Veterans Affairs
VA Regional Loan Center
Box 25126
Denver, CO 80225
888-349-7541

ARIZONA OFFICE
Jurisdiction: Arizona, California, Nevada

Department of Veterans Affairs
VA Regional Loan Center
3225 N. Central Ave.
Phoenix, AZ 85012
888-869-0194

NEW YORK OFFICES
Buffalo

Jurisdiction: NY Counties of Allegany, Cattaraugus, Chautaugua, Erie, Genesee, Livingston, Monroe, Niagara, Ontario, Orleans, Steuben, Wayne, Wyoming, Yates

Department of Veterans Affairs
VA Regional Loan Center
111 West Huron St.
Buffalo, NY 14202
716-662-5293

New York City

Jurisdiction: All Counties not listed under Buffalo

Department of Veterans Affairs
VA Regional Loan Center
245 W. Houston St.
New York, NY 10014
212-807-7229

Appendix C
Fannie Mae Designated Central Cities

Home buyers may be eligible for FannieNeighbors if the home they wish to purchase is located in one of the following designated central cities.

Fannie Mae recognizes the following list of central cities as designated by the U.S. Office of Management and Budget, dated June 1993, and updated June 30, 1995.

1-800-7-FANNIE (800-732-6643)

The following two web addresses will be helpful in not only locating a home to purchase, but also in locating a lender
http://www.fanniemae.com/homes/index.html
www.homepath.com/hls1.html

Disclaimer: Lenders listed in the HomePath site are separate and independent from Fannie Mae. The listing of a lender does not in any way indicate that Fannie Mae endorses, sponsors, or reviews the information provided by a particular lender. Searching for a lender above indicates your acknowledgment that you have read and accept this disclaimer.

ALABAMA

Anniston
Birmingham
Decatur
Dothan
Florence
Gadsden
Huntsville
Mobile
Montgomery
Tuscaloosa

ALASKA

Anchorage

ARIZONA

Flagstaff
Mesa
Phoenix
Scottsdale
Tempe
Tucson
Yuma

ARKANSAS

Conway
Fayetteville
Fort Smith
Jacksonville
Little Rock
North Little Rock
Pine Bluff
Rogers
Springdale
Texarkana
West Memphis

CALIFORNIA

Alameda
Anaheim
Atascadero
Bakersfield
Berkeley
Chico
Coronado
Davis
El Paso de Robles
Escondido
Fairfield
Fresno
Gilroy
Hemet
Irvine
Lancaster
Lodi
Lompoc
Long Beach
Los Angeles
Madera
Merced
Modesto
Monterey

Appendix C (cont.)
Fannie Mae Designated Central Cities

Napa
Oakland
Palm Desert
Palm Springs
Palo Alto
Paradise
Pasadena
Petaluma
Porterville
Redding
Riverside
Sacramento
Salinas
Oakland
Palm Desert
Palm Springs
Palo Alto
Paradise
Pasadena
Petaluma
Porterville
Redding
Riverside
Sacramento
Salinas
San Bernadino
San Buenaventura
San Diego
San Francisco
San Jose
San Luis Obispo
Santa Ana
Santa Barbara
Santa Clara
Santa Cruz
Santa Maria
Santa Rosa
Stockton
Sunnyvale
Temecula
Tulare
Turlock
Vallejo
Visalia
Watsonville
Woodland
Yuba City

COLORADO

Boulder
Colorado Springs
Denver
Fort Collins
Grand Junction
Greeley
Longmont
Loveland
Pueblo

CONNECTICUT

Bridgeport
Danbury
Hartford
Meriden
Middletown
New Haven
New London
Norwalk
Norwich
Stamford
Waterbury

DELAWARE

Dover
Newark
Wilmington

DISTRICT OF COLUMBIA

Washington

FLORIDA

Boca Raton
Bradenton
Cape Coral
Clearwater
Daytona Beach
Fort Lauderdale
Fort Meyers
Fort Pierce
Fort Walton Beach

Appendix C (cont.)
Fannie Mae Designated Central Cities

Gainesville
Jacksonville
Lakeland
Melbourne
Miami
Miami Beach
Naples
Ocala
Orlando
Palm Bay
Panama City
Pensacola
Port St. Lucie
Punta Gorda
St. Petersburg
Sarasota
Tallahassee
Tampa
Titusville
West Palm Beach
Winter Haven

GEORGIA

Albany
Athens-Clarke County
Atlanta
Augusta
Columbus
Macon
Savannah

HAWAII

Honolulu

IDAHO

Boise City
Nampa

ILLINOIS

Alton
Aurora
Belleville
Bloomington
Champaign
Chicago
Decatur
Dekalb
East St. Louis
Elgin
Evanston
Granite City
Joliet
Kankakee
Moline
Normal
North Chicago
Pekin
Peoria
Rock Island
Rockford
Springfield
Urbana

INDIANA

Anderson
Bloomington
East Chicago
Elkhart
Evansville
Fort Wayne
Gary
Goshen
Indianapolis
Kokomo
Lafayette
Muncie
New Albany
South Bend
Terre Haute

IOWA

Cedar Falls
Cedar Rapids
Council Bluffs
Davenport
Des Moines
Dubuque

Appendix C (cont.)
Fannie Mae Designated Central Cities

Iowa City
Sioux Falls
Waterloo

KANSAS

Kansas City
Lawrence
Leavenworth
Olathe
Topeka
Wichita

KENTUCKY

Ashland
Henderson
Hopkinsville
Lexington-Fayette
Louisville
Owensboro

LOUISIANA

Alexandria
Baton Rouge
Bossier City
Houma
Lafayette
Lake Charles
Monroe
New Orleans
Shreveport
Slidell

MAINE

Auburn
Bangor
Lewiston
Portland

MARYLAND

Annapolis
Baltimore
Cumberland
Frederick
Hagerstown

MASSACHUSETTS

Attleboro
Barnstable
Boston
Brockton
Cambridge
Fall River
Fitchburg
Gloucester
Holyoke
Lawrence
Leominster
Lowell
Lynn
New Bedford
Northampton
Pittsfield
Springfield
Waltham
Westfield
Worcester
Yarmouth

MICHIGAN

Ann Arbor
Battle Creek
Bay City
Benton Harbor
Dearborn
Detroit
East Lansing
Flint
Grand Rapids
Holland
Jackson
Kalamazoo
Lansing
Midland
Muskegon
Pontiac
Port Huron
Saginaw

Appendix C (cont.)
Fannie Mae Designated Central Cities

MINNESOTA
Duluth
Minneapolis
Moorhead
Rochester
St. Cloud
St. Paul

MISSISSIPPI
Biloxi
Gulfport
Hattiesburg
Jackson
Pascagoula

MISSOURI
Columbia
Joplin
Kansas City
Springfield
St. Charles
St. Joseph
St. Louis

MONTANA
Billings
Great Falls

NEBRASKA
Lincoln
Omaha

NEVADA
Las Vegas
Reno

NEW HAMPSHIRE
Manchester
Nashua
Portsmouth
Rochester

NEW JERSEY
Atlantic City
Bayonne
Bridgeton
Camden
Dover Township
Jersey City
Millville
Newark
Trenton
Vineland

NEW MEXICO
Albuquerque
Las Cruces
Santa Fe

NEW YORK
Albany
Auburn
Binghamton
Buffalo
Elmira
Glens Falls
Jamestown
New York
Newburgh
Niagara Falls
Poughkeepsie
Rochester
Rome
Saratoga Springs
Schenectady
Syracuse
Troy
Utica
White Plains

Appendix C (cont.)
Fannie Mae Designated Central Cities

NORTH CAROLINA
Asheville
Burlington
Chapel Hill
Charlotte
Concord
Durham
Fayatteville
Gastonia
Greensboro
Greenville
Hickory
High Point
Jacksonville
Kannapolis
Morgenton
Raleigh
Rocky Mount
Wilmington
Winston-Salem

NORTH DAKOTA
Bismarck
Fargo
Grand Forks

OHIO
Akron
Bowling Green
Canton
Cincinnati
Cleveland
Columbus
Dayton
Elyria
Fairborn
Hamilton
Kent
Lancaster
Lima
Lorain
Mansfield
Marietta
Massillon
Middletown
Newark
Springfield
Steubenville
Toledo
Warren
Youngstown

OKLAHOMA
Enid
Lawton
Norman
Oklahoma City
Shawnee
Tulsa

OREGON
Ashland
Eugene
Medford
Portland
Salem
Springfield

PENNSYLVANIA
Allentown
Altoona
Bethlehem
Carlisle
Erie
Harrisburg
Johnstown
Lancaster
Lebanon
Philadelphia
Pittsburgh
Reading
Scranton
Sharon
State College
WilkesBarre
Williamsport
York

Appendix C (cont.)
Fannie Mae Designated Central Cities

PUERTO RICO
Aguadilla
Arecibo
Bayamon
Caguas
Cayey
Fajardo
Humacao
Manati
Mayaguez
Ponce
San Juan
Vega Baja

RHODE ISLAND
Pawtucket
Providence
Warwick
Woonsocket

SOUTH CAROLINA
Aiken
Anderson
Charleston
Columbia
Florence
Greenville
Myrtle Beach
North Charleston
Rock Hill
Spartanburg
Sumter

SOUTH DAKOTA
Rapid City
Sioux Falls

TENNESSEE
Bristol
Chattanooga
Clarksville
Jackson
Johnson City
Kingsport
Knoxville
Memphis
Murfreesboro
Nashville-Davidson
Oak Ridge

TEXAS
Abilene
Amarillo
Arlington
Austin
Baytown
Beaumont
Brownsville
Bryan
College Station
Conroe
Corpus Christi
Dallas
Denison
Denton
Edinburg
El Paso
Fort Worth
Galveston
Harlingen
Houston
Irving
Killeen
Laredo
Longview
Lubbock
Marshall
McAllen
Midland
Mission
New Braunfels
Odessa
Port Arthur
San Angelo
San Antonio
San Benito
San Marcos

Appendix C (cont.)
Fannie Mae Designated Central Cities

Sherman
Temple
Texarkana
Texas City
Tyler
Victoria
Waco
Wichita Falls

UTAH

Clearfield
Ogden
Orem
Provo
Salt Lake City

VERMONT

Burlington

VIRGINIA

Arlington
Bristol
Charlottesville
Danville
Fredericksburg
Hampton
Lynchburg
Newport News
Norfolk
Petersburg
Portsmouth
Richmond
Roanoke
Suffolk
Virginia Beach

WASHINGTON

Bellevue
Bellingham
Bremerton
Everett
Kennewick
Olympia
Pasco
Richland
Seattle
Spokane
Tacoma
Vancouver
Yakima

WEST VIRGINIA

Charleston
Huntington
Parkersburg
Weirton
Wheeling

WISCONSIN

Appleton
Beloit
Eau Claire
Green Bay
Janesville
Kenosha
La Crosse
Madison
Milwaukee
Neenah
Oshkosh
Racine
Sheboygan
Superior
Waukesha
Wausau

WYOMING

Casper
Cheyenne

Appendix D
Internal Revenue Service

The IRS has changed their method of handling sales of seized Personal Property (Real-Estate Foreclosures and vehicle auctions). As the number of the sales has decreased in recent months, this agency is now listing them on a national rather than local basis.

The United States Treasury had set up an automated Hot Line for anyone interested in Information concerning these sales. This 24-hour automated telephone information service provides callers with immediate information on auctions throughout the United States and Puerto Rico. Convenient and easy to use, the Public Auction Line provides details on upcoming sales including sale dates and times, locations, and an overview of the merchandise for sale.

The US Treasury Department also maintains a convenient website at:

http://www.treas.gov/auctions/

A wealth of information can be found at this website. We encourage you to check this out as well as their handy search tool located at:

http://www.treas.gov/Architext/AT-allquery.html

Public Auction Line: 703-273-3441 x234

Appendix E
State Surplus Offices

ALABAMA
Alabama Surplus Property
P.O. Box 210487
Montgomery, AL 36121
334-277-5866
www.state.al.us/
(search Dept. of Public Safety)

ALASKA
Surplus Property Management Office
2400 Viking Dr.
Anchorage, AK 99501
907-279-0596
907-465-2250 - Juneau office
907-465-2250 - *Mailing list*
www.state.ak.us/cgi-bin/qsearch.cgi

ARIZONA
Office of Surplus Property
1537 W. Jackson St.
Phoenix, AZ 85007
602-542-5701

ARKANSAS
State Marketing & Redistribution Office
6620 Young Rd.
Little Rock, AR 72209
501-565-8645 - *Mailing list*

CALIFORNIA
Office of Fleet Administration
802 Q St.
Sacramento, CA 95814
916-327-2085
http://www.ofa.dgs.ca.gov/services/auction.asp

COLORADO
Department of Correctional Industries
State Surplus Agency
4200 Garfield St.
Denver, CO 80216
303-321-4012 - *Mailing list*
www.cijvp.com

CONNECTICUT
Surplus Property contracts out to:
Clearing House Auction Galleries
207 Church St.
Wethersfield, CT 06109
860-529-3344
www.clearinghouseauctions.com

DELAWARE
Division of Purchasing
Surplus Property
P.O. Box 299
Delaware City, DE 19706
302-834-4550 - *vehicles, office furniture and other surplus property.*
www.state.de.us/purchase/

DISTRICT OF COLUMBIA
Department of Public Works
5001 Shepard Parkway
Washington, DC 20032
202-576-7850 or 576-6472
No mailing list. Registration fee.

FLORIDA
Department of Management Services
904-488-5272
Motor Vehicle Bureau
904-488-5178 - *holds vehicle auctions once a month at various locations throughout the state.*

Appendix E (cont.)
State Surplus Offices

GEORGIA

Department of Administrative Services
Purchasing Division, Surplus Property
1050 Murphy Ave. South West Bldg. 12
Atlanta, GA 30310
404-756-4800 - *Mailing list*
www.dos.state.ga.us

HAWAII

City Hall
530 S. King St., Rm. 115
Honolulu, HI 96813
808-527-6789
www.co.honolulu.hi.us

IDAHO

Division of Purchasing
5569 Kendall
Boise, ID 83706
208-334-3477
www.state.id.us./adm/purchasing/
Idaho's state agencies hold their own auctions. You must contact the specific state agency directly. Auctions are advertised in local newspapers.

ILLINOIS

Central Management Services
Division of Property Control
3550 Great Northern Ave.
Springfield, IL 62707
217-785-6903

INDIANA

State Surplus Property Section
229 W. New York St.
Indianapolis, IN 46202
317-591-5320

IOWA

Department of Natural Resources
Wallace State Office Bldg.
Des Moines, IA 50319
515-281-5121

KANSAS

State Surplus Property
P.O. Box 19226
Topeka, KS 66619-0226
913-296-2334

KENTUCKY

Office of Surplus Property
514 Barrett Ave.
Frankfurt, KY 40601
502-564-4836 - *Mailing list*
www.state.ky.us/agencies/adm/mars/auction.htm

LOUISIANA

Division of Administration
Louisiana Property Assistance Agency
P.O. Box 94095
1502 N. 17th St.
Baton Rouge, LA 70804

MAINE

Office of Surplus Property
Station 95
Augusta, ME 04333
207-287-2923 *No mailing list*
www.janus.state.me.us/purchase/surplus/surplus.htm

MARYLAND

Office of Surplus Property
P.O. Box 1039
8037 Brock Ridge Rd.
Jessup, MD 20794
410-799-0440

Appendix E (cont.)
State Surplus Offices

MASSACHUSETTS
State Purchasing Agency
Department of Procurement
& General Services
Surplus Property
One Ashburton Place
Boston, MA 02108
617-720-3380 *No mailing list*

MICHIGAN
Department of Management & Budget
State Surplus Property
P.O. Box 30026
Lansing, MI 48913
517-335-8444 - *Mailing list*
www.state.mi.us/dmb/dir/auction.htm

MINNISOTA
Surplus Operations Office
5420 Highway 8
Arden Hills, MN 55112
651-639-4022
www.mmd.admin.state.mn.us

MISSISSIPPI
Bureau of Surplus Property
P.O. Box 5778
Jackson, MS 39288
601-939-2050 - *Mailing list*

MISSOURI
Surplus Property Office
Materials Management Section
P.O. Drawer 1310
Jefferson City, MO 65102
573-751-3415 - *Mailing list*
www.oa.state.mo.us/purch/
surplus.html

MONTANA
Property and Supply Bureau
930 Lyndale Ave.
Helena, MT 59620
406-444-4514 x126 - *Mailing list*
www.state.mt.us/

NEBRASKA
Office of Administrative Services
Material Division,
Surplus Property
P.O. Box 94901
Lincoln, NE 68509
402-479-4890 - *Mailing list*
www.state.ne.us
www.nol.org/home/DASMAT/
sp.htm

NEVADA
State Purchasing Division
Kinkead Building
400 Capitol Complex
Carson City, NV 89710
702-687-4070 - *Mailing list*
Separate sealed bid auction. You must bid at least once over two to three auctions or you'll be dropped from the list.

NEW HAMPSHIRE
Office of Surplus Property
144 Clinton St.
Concord, NH 03301
603-271-3241 - *Mailing list*

NEW JERSEY
Purchase and Property
Distribution Center
P.O. Box 234
Trenton, NJ 08625
609-292-9694
www.state.nj.us/treasury/dss/
csdssauc.htm

Appendix E (cont.)
State Surplus Offices

NEW MEXICO
Highway & Transportation Department
P.O. Box 1149
Santa Fe, NM 87504
505-827-5587 - *Mailing list*
Last Saturday in September. Vehicles and office equipment.

NEW YORK
Office of General Services
Bureau of Surplus Property
Bldg. #18, Har riman State Office Bldg.
Albany, NY 12226
518-457-6335
www.ogs.state.ny.us/surpluspublic/default.htm

NORTH CAROLINA
State Surplus Property
P.O. Box 33900
Raleigh, NC 27636
919-733-3889 - *Mailing list*
Fax: 919-733-9573
Sealed bid auctions. Warehouse available to inspect items.
E-mail: maryalice.sechler@ncmail.net
www.doa.state.nc.us/ssp/ssp.htm

NORTH DAKOTA
Surplus Property Office
P.O. Box 7293
Bismarck, ND 58507
701-328-2543

OHIO
State and Federal Surplus Property
4200 Surface Rd.
Columbus, OH 43228
614-466-5052
www.state.oh.us/das/gsd/surplus/sfsur.html

OKLAHOMA
Purchasing Department
3301 N. Santa Fe
Oklahoma City, OK 73105
405-521-2206 - *Mailing list*

OREGON
Department of General Services
Surplus Property
1655 Salem Industrial Dr. N.E.
Salem, OR 97310
503-378-4714
www.oregonsurplus.com

PENNSYLVANIA
General Services Department
Bureau of Vehicle Management
2221 Forster St.
Harrisburg, PA 17105
717-783-3132 - *Mailing list*
www.dgs.state.pa.us/auction.htm

RHODE ISLAND
Department of Administration
Division of Purchase
1 Capitol Hill
Providence, RI 02908

SOUTH CAROLINA
Surplus Property Office
Division of General Services
1441 Boston Ave.
West Columbia, SC 29170
803-896-6880
www.ogs.state.sc.us/disposable/DPO-auction2000.html

SOUTH DAKOTA
Bureau of Administration
State Property Management
1320 E. Sioux Ave.
Pierre, SD 57501
605-773-4935
www.state.sd.us

Appendix E (cont.)
State Surplus Offices

TENNESSEE
Department of General Services
Property Utilization Division
6500 Centennial Blvd.
Nashville, TN 37243
615-350-3373 - *Mailing list*
www.state.tn.us/generalserv/ba04s

TEXAS
State Purchasing & General
Services Commission
P.O. Box 13047 Capitol Station
Austin, TX 78711
512-463-3381
www.state.tx.us

UTAH
State Surplus Office
522 S. 700 West
Salt Lake City, UT 84104
801-533-5885
http://dasdgs.state.ut.us

VERMONT
Surplus Property
375 River St.
Montpelier, VT 05602
802-828-3394
www.state.vt.us

VIRGINIA
State Surplus Property
P.O. Box 1199
Richmond, VA 23231
804-236-3666

WASHINGTON
Surplus Property
1222 46th Ave. East
Fife, WA 98424
253-597-3734
www.ga.wa.gov/surplus/
surplus.htm

WEST VIRGINIA
State Agency Surplus Property
2700 Charles Ave.
Dunbar, WV 25064
304-766-2626
www.state.wv.us/admin/
purchase/surplus

WISCONSIN
Department of Transportation
P.O. Box 7880
Madison, WI 53707
608-266-1719

WYOMING
State Motor Pool
723 W. 19th St.
Cheyenne, WY 82002
307-777-6855

Appendix F
Small Business Administration District Offices

ALASKA

222 W. 8th Ave.
Anchorage, AK 99513-7559
907-271-4022
Fax: 907-271-4545
www.sba.gov/regions/states/ak/indexabout.html

ALABAMA

2121 8th Ave. North
Birmingham, AL 35203-2398
205-731-1344
Fax: 205-731-1404
www.sba.gov/regions/states/al/indexabout.html

ARIZONA

2828 N. Central Ave.
Phoenix, AZ 85004-1093
602-745-7200
Fax: 602-745-7210
www.sba.gov/regions/states/az/

CALIFORNIA

Fresno
2719 N. Air Fresno Dr., Suite 200
Fresno, CA 93727
559-487-5791
800-359-1833, *press 6*
Fax: 559-487-5636
www.sba.gov/regions/states/ca/fresno/fdoabout.html

Los Angeles
330 N. Brand, Suite 1200
Glendale, CA 91203
818-552-3210
www.sba.gov/regions/states/ca/la/indexabout.html

Sacramento
660 J St., Suite 215
Sacramento, CA 95814
916-498-6410
Fax: 916-498-6422
www.sba.gov/regions/states/ca/sacr/indexabout.html

San Diego
550 W. "C" St., Suite 550
San Diego, CA 92101-3500
619-557-7250
Fax: 619-557-5894
www.sba.gov/regions/states/ca/sandiego/indexabout.html

Santa Ana
200 W. Santa Ana Blvd.
Santa Ana, CA 92701
714-550-7420
Fax: 714-550-0191
TTY: 714-550-0655
www.sba.gov/regions/states/ca/santa/aboutsant.html

COLORADO

721 19th St., Suite 426
Denver, CO 80202
303-844-2607
Fax: 303-844-6468
www.sba.gov/regions/states/co/indexabout.html

CONNECTICUT

330 Main St., 2nd Floor
Hartford, CT 06106
860-240-4700
Fax: 860-240-4659
TTD: 860-524-1611
www.sba.gov/regions/states/ct/ctdobout.html

Appendix F (cont.)
Small Business Administration District Offices

DELAWARE
824 N. Market St.
Wilmington, DE 19801-3011
302-573-6294
Fax: 302-573-6060
www.sba.gov/regions/states/de/

DISTRICT OF COLUMBIA
1110 Vermont Ave., NW
9th Floor
Washington, D.C. 20005
202-606-4000
www.sba.gov/regions/states/dc/

FLORIDA
North Florida
7825 Baymeadows Way, Suite 100B
Jacksonville, FL 32256
904-443-1900
Fax: 904-443-1980
TTY: 904-443-1909
www.sba.gov/regions/states/fl/north/

South Florida
100 S. Biscayne Blvd., 7th Floor
Miami, FL 33131
305-536-5521
Fax: 305-536-5058
www.sba.gov/regions/states/fl/south/
indexabout.html

GEORGIA
Harris Tower
233 Peachtree St. NE
Atlanta, GA 30303
404-331-0100
404-331-1900
Fax: 404-331-0101
www.sba.gov/regions/states/ga/

HAWAII
300 Ala Moana Blvd.
Rm. 2-235
Box 50207
Honolulu, HI 96850
808-541-2981
Fax: 808-541-2976
www.sba.gov/regions/states/hi/

IDAHO
1020 Main St.
Boise, ID 83702
208-334-1696
Fax: 208-334-9353
www.sba.gov/regions/states/id/

ILLINOIS
500 W. Madison St., Suite 1250
Chicago, IL 60661-2511
312-353-4528
Fax: 312-886-5688
www.sba.gov/regions/states/il/

INDIANA
429 N. Pennsylvania St.
Suite 100
Indianapolis, IN 46204-1873
317-226-7272
Fax: 317-226-7259
www.sba.gov/regions/states/in/
indobout.html

IOWA
Cedar Rapids
215 4th Ave. SE
Cedar Rapids, IA 52401
319-362-6405
Fax: 319-362-7861
www.sba.gov/regions/states/ia/
crmap.html

Appendix F (cont.)
Small Business Administration District Offices

Des Moines
210 Walnut St., Rm. 749
Des Moines, IA 50309
515-284-4422
www.sba.gov/regions/states/ia/desmo/desmmap.html

KANSAS
271 W. Third St. North
Suite 2500
Wichita, KS 67202-1212
316-269-6616
Fax: 316-269-6499
www.sba.gov/regions/states/ks/

KENTUCKY
The Romano Mazzoli Federal Building
600 Dr. MLK Jr. Place
Louisville, KY 40202
502-582-5761
www.sba.gov/regions/states/ky/indexabout.html

LOUISIANA
365 Canal St.
New Orleans, LA 70130
504-589-6685
Fax: 504-589-2339
www.sba.gov/regions/states/la/indexabout.html

MAINE
40 Western Ave.
Augusta, ME 04330
207-622-8274
Fax: 207-622-8277
www.sba.gov/regions/states/me/

MARYLAND
10 S. Howard St.
Baltimore, MD 21201-2525
410-962-4392
Fax: 410-962-1805
www.sba.gov/regions/states/md/indexabout.html

MASSACHUSETTS
1093 10 Causeway St., Rm. 265
Boston, MA 02222
617-565-5590
Fax: 617-565-5598
www.sba.gov/regions/states/ma/indexabout.html

MICHIGAN
477 Michigan Ave., Suite 515
McNamara Building
Detroit, MI 48226
313-226-6075
Fax: 313-226-4769
e-mail: michigan@sba.gov
www.sba.gov/regions/states/mi/indexabout.html

MINNESOTA
100 N. 6th St.
Minneapolis, MN 55403-1563
612-370-2324
Fax: 612-370-2303
www.sba.gov/regions/states/mn/St.html

MISSISSIPPI
101 Capital Center
101 W. Capitol St., Suite 400
Jackson, MS 39201
601-965-4378
Fax: 601-965-4294
www.sba.gov/regions/states/ms/indexabout.html

Appendix F (cont.)
Small Business Administration District Offices

MISSOURI

Kansas City
323 W. 8th St., Suite 501
Kansas City, MO 64105
816-374-6708
Fax: 816-374-6759
www.sba.gov/regions/states/mo/kansas/ksmomap.htm

St. Louis
815 Olive St., Rm. 242
St. Louis, MO 63101
314-539-6600
Fax: 314-539-3785
www.sba.gov/regions/states/mo/stlmap.html

MONTANA

Federal Building
301 S. Park, Rm. 334
Drawer 10054
Helena, MT 59626
406 441-1081
800-776-9144, *press 2*
www.sba.gov/regions/states/mt/

NEBRASKA

11145 Mill Valley Rd.
Omaha, NE 68154
402-221-4691
Fax: 402-221-3680
www.sba.gov/regions/states/ne/indexabout.html

NEVADA

300 Las Vegas Blvd. South
Suite 1100
Las Vegas, NV 89101
702-388-6611
Fax: 702-388-6469
www.sba.gov/regions/states/nv/indexabout.html

NEW HAMPSHIRE

143 N. Main St.
Concord, NH 03301
603-225-1400
Fax: 603-225-1409
www.sba.gov/regions/states/nh/indexabout.html

NEW JERSEY

Two Gateway Center
15th Floor
Newark, NJ 07102
973-645-2434
www.sba.gov/regions/states/nj/

NEW MEXICO

625 Silver Ave., SW
Albuquerque, NM 87102
505-346-7909
Fax: 505-346-6711
www.sba.gov/regions/states/nm/indexabout.html

NEW YORK

Buffalo
111 W. Huron St., Suite 1311
Buffalo, NY 14202
716-551-4301
Fax: 716-551-4418
www.sba.gov/regions/states/ny/buffalo/indexabout.html

New York City
26 Federal Plaza, Suite 3100
New York, NY 10278
212-264-4354
www.sba.gov/regions/states/ny/ny/

Appendix F (cont.)
Small Business Administration District Offices

NORTH CAROLINA
200 N. College St., Suite A-2015
Charlotte, NC 28202
704-344-6563
Fax: 704-344-6769
www.sba.gov/regions/states/nc/indexabout.html

NORTH DAKOTA
657 Second Ave. North, Rm. 219
Fargo, ND 58108
701-239-5131
www.sba.gov/regions/states/nd/

OHIO
Cleveland
1111 Superior Ave.
Cleveland, OH 44114-2507
216-522-4180
Fax: 216-522-2038
www.sba.gov/regions/states/oh/cleveland/indexabout.html

Columbus
25922 Nationwide Plaza
Columbus, OH 43215
614-469-6860
Fax: 614-469-2391
www.sba.gov/regions/states/oh/columbus/

OKLAHOMA
210 Park Ave., Suite 1300
Oklahoma City, OK 73102
405-231-5521
Fax: 405-231-4876
www.sba.gov/regions/states/ok/

OREGON
1515 SW Fifth Ave., Suite 1050
Portland, OR 97201-5494
503-326-2682
Fax: 503-326-2808
www.sba.gov/regions/states/or/ormap.html

PENNSYLVANIA
Philadelphia
Robert N.C. Nix Federal Building
900 Market St., 5th Floor
Philadelphia, PA 19107
215-580-2SBA (215-580-2722)
Fax: 215-580-2762
TTY: 215-580-2757
www.sba.gov/regions/states/pa/phil/

Pittsburgh
Federal Building, Rm. 1128
1000 Liberty Ave.
Pittsburgh, PA 15222
412-395-6560
Fax: 412-395-6562
www.sba.gov/regions/states/pa/pitt/

RHODE ISLAND
380 Westminster St.
Providence, RI 02903
401-528-4562
Fax: 401-528-4539
www.sba.gov/regions/states/ri/ridobout.html

SOUTH CAROLINA
1835 Assembly St., Rm. 358
Columbia, SC 29201
803-765-5377
www.sba.gov/regions/states/sc/

Appendix F (cont.)
Small Business Administration District Offices

SOUTH DAKOTA
110 S. Phillips Ave., Suite 200
Sioux Falls, SD 57104-6721
605-330-4243 x26
www.sba.gov/regions/states/sd/

TENNESSEE
50 Vantage Way, Suite 201
Nashville, TN 37228
615-736-5881
www.sba.gov/regions/states/tn/
nashmap.html

TEXAS
Dallas/Fort Worth
4300 Amon Carter Blvd. Suite 114
Fort Worth, TX 75155
817-885-6500
Fax: 817-885-6516
www.sba.gov/regions/states/tx/dallas/

El Paso
10737 Gateway West
El Paso, TX 79935
915-633-7001
Fax: 915-633-7005
www.sba.gov/regions/states/tx/elpaso/
indexabout.html

Harlingen
222 E. Van Buren, Suite 500
Harlingen, TX 78550
956-427-8533
Fax: 956-427-8537
www.sba.gov/regions/states/tx/
harlingen/indexabout.html

Corpus Christi
606 N. Carancahua, Suite 1200
Corpus Christi, TX 78476
361-888-3331
Fax: 361-888-3418

Houston
9301 SW Freeway
Houston, TX 77074-1591
713-773-6500
Fax: 713-773-6550

Lubbock
1205 Texas Ave., Suite 408
Lubbock, TX 79401-2693
806-472-7462
Fax: 806-472-7487

UTAH
125 S. State St., Rm. 2231
Salt Lake City, UT 84138
801-524-3209
Fax: 801-524-4160 or 4410
www.sba.gov/regions/states/ut/
about5.html

VERMONT
87 State St.
Montpelier, VT 05601
802-828-4422
Fax: 802-828-4485
www.sba.gov/regions/states/vt/
vtlocalmap.html

VIRGINIA
400 N. 8th St., Suite 1150
Richmond, VA 23240
804-771-2400
www.sba.gov/regions/states/va/
rdodirec.html

WASHINGTON
Seattle
1200 6th Ave., Suite 1700
Seattle, WA 98101-1128
206-553-7310
Fax: 206-553-7099
www.sba.gov/regions/states/wa/s

Appendix F (cont.)
Small Business Administration District Offices

Spokane
801 W. Riverside Ave.
Suite 200
Spokane, WA 99201-0901
509-353-2800
Fax: 509-353-2829

WEST VIRGINIA

320 W. Pike St., Suite 330
Clarksburg, WV 26301
304-623-5631
www.sba.gov/regions/states/wv/

WISCONSIN

Madison
740 Regent St., Suite 100
Madison, WI 53715
608-264-5261
Fax: 608-264-5541
TTY: 608-264-5516.

Milwaukee
310 W. Wisconsin Ave.
Suite 400
Milwaukee, WI 53203
414-297-3941
Fax: 414-297-1377
TTY: 414-297-1095
www.sba.gov/regions/states/wi/
indexabout.html

WYOMING

100 E. B St., Rm. 4001
Box 2839
Casper, WY 82602
307-261-6500
Fax: 307-261-6535
www.sba.gov/regions/states/wy/
indexabout.html

Appendix G
Bureau of Land Management State Offices

Check website at: www.blm.gov/nhp/browse.htm

ALASKA

222 W. 7th Ave., #13
Anchorage, AK 99513-7599
907-271-5960
http://www.ak.blm.gov/

Anchorage Field Office
6881 Abbott Loop Rd.
Anchorage, AK 99507-2599
907-267-1246
(toll free only within Alaska)
www.anchorage.ak.blm.gov/

Glennallen Field Office
P.O. Box 147
Glennallen, AK 99588
907-822-3217
www.glennallen.ak.blm.gov/
gdolands.html

ARIZONA

Arizona State Office
222 N. Central Ave.
Phoenix, AZ 85004-2203
602-417-9200
Fax: 602-417-9556
www.az.blm.gov/

Kingman Field Office
2475 Beverly Ave.
Kingman, AZ 86401-3629
520-692-4400
Fax: 520-692-4414
kingman.az.blm.gov/Kfohome1.htm

Tucson Field Office
12661 East Broadway
Tucson, AZ 85748-7208
520-722-4289
Fax: 520-751-0948
tucson.az.blm.gov/tfo.html

CALIFORNIA

California State Office
2800 Cottage Way, Rm. W-1834
Sacramento, CA 95825-1886
916-978-4400
TTY: 916- 978-4419
www.ca.blm.gov/caso/
index.html

California Desert District Office
6221 Box Springs Blvd.
Riverside, CA 92507
909-697-5200
www.ca.blm.gov/cdd/

Redding Field Office
355 Hemsted Dr.
Redding, CA 96002
530-224-2100
www.ca.blm.gov/redding/

COLORADO

2850 Youngfield St.
Lakewood, CO 80215-7076
303-239-3600
www.co.blm.gov/

Grand Junction Field Office
2815 H Rd.
Grand Junction, CO 81506
970-244-3000
Fax: 970-244-3083
www.co.blm.gov/gjra/gjra.html

San Juan Field Office USFS/BLM
Calvin Joyner
15 Burnett Court
Durango, CO 81301
970-247-4874
Fax: 970-385-1375
www.co.blm.gov/sjra/sjra.html

Appendix G (cont.)

Bureau of Land Management State Offices

Little Snake Field Office
John Husband
455 Emerson St.
Craig, CO 81625
970-826-5000
Fax: 970-826-5002
www.co.blm.gov/lsra/lsraindex.htm

STATES EAST OF THE MISSISSIPPI RIVER, plus ARKANSAS, IOWA, LOUISIANA, MINNESOTA, and MISSOURI

Eastern States Office
7450 Boston Blvd.
Springfield, VA 22153
703-440-1600
703-440-1727 -Information
www.es.blm.gov/index.html

Jackson Field Office
411 Briarwood Dr., Suite 404
Jackson, MS 39206
601-977-0730

Milwaukee Field Office
310 West Wisconsin Ave., Suite 450
Milwaukee, WI 53203
414-297-4400

IDAHO

Idaho State Office
1387 South Vinnell Way
Boise, ID 83709-1657
208-373-4000 - Information
www.id.blm.gov/

Lower Snake River District
3948 Development Ave.
Boise, ID 83705
208-384-3300 - Information

Pocatello Field Office
1111 N 8th Ave.
Pocatello, ID 83201-5789
208-478-6340 - Information

MONTANA, NORTH DAKOTA, and SOUTH DAKOTA

5001 Southgate Dr.
P.O. Box 36800
Billings, MT 59107
406-896-5013
Fax: 406-896-5301
E-mail: bifoinfo@mt.blm.gov
www.mt.blm.gov/

Butte Field Office
106 N. Parkmont
Butte, MT 59701
P.O. Box 3388
Butte, MT 59702-3388
406-494-5059
Fax: 406-494-3474
E-mail: bzinfo@mt.blm.gov

North Dakota Field Office
2933 Third Ave. West
Dickinson, ND 58601-2619
701-225-9148
Fax: 701-227-8510
E-mail: ndfoinfo@mt.blm.gov

South Dakota Field Office
310 Roundup St.
Belle Fourche, SD 57717-1698
605-892-2526
Fax: 605-892-4742
E-mail: sdfoinfo@mt.blm.gov

NEVADA

Battle Mountain Field Office
50 Bastian Rd.
Battle Mountain, NV
89820-1420
http://www.nv.blm.gov/
bmountain/

Appendix G (cont.)
Bureau of Land Management State Offices

Carson City Field Office
5665 Morgan Mill Rd.
Carson City, NV 89701-1448
775-885-6000
Fax: 775-885-6147
www.nv.blm.gov/carson/default.htm

Las Vegas Office
4765 W. Vegas Dr.
Las Vegas, NV 89108-2135
702-647-5000
Fax: 702-647-5023
www.nv.blm.gov/vegas/default.htm

NEW MEXICO, KANSAS, OKLAHOMA, and TEXAS

1474 Rodeo Rd.
P.O. Box 27115
Santa Fe, NM 87502-0115
505-438-7400
Fax: 505-438-7435
State Tracts Sales: 512 475-1427
www.nm.blm.gov/www/directory.html

Albuquerque Field Office
435 Montano Rd., NE
Albuquerque, NM 87107-4935
505-761-8700
Fax: 505-761-8911
www.nm.blm.gov/www/afo/afo_home.html

Amarillo Field Office
801 S. Fillmore St., Suite 500
Amarillo, TX 79101-3545
806-324-2617
Fax: 806-324-2633
www.nm.blm.gov/www/amfo/amfo_home.html

Lufkin Inspection Office
Homer Garrison Federal Building
701 N. 1st. Rm. 106
Lufkin, TX 75901
409-639-4108
Fax: 409-639-8693

Tulsa Field Office
7906 E. 33rd St., Suite 101
Tulsa, OK 74145-1352
918-621-4100
Fax: 918-621-4130
www.nm.blm.gov/www/tufo/tufo_home.html

OREGON and WASHINGTON

State Office
1515 SW 5th Ave.
P.O. Box 2965
Portland, OR 97208-2965
503-952-6002
Fax: 503-952-6308
TTY: 503-952-6372
E-mail: or912mb@or.blm.gov
www.or.blm.gov/orwadir.htm

Burns District Office
HC 74-12533, Hwy 20 West
Hines, OR 97738
541-573-4400
Fax: 541-573-4411

Coos Bay District Office
1300 Airport Lane
North Bend, OR 97459
541-756-0100
Fax: 541-756-9303

Wenatchee Resource Area
915 N. Walla Walla
Wenatchee, WA 98801
509-665-2100
Fax: 509-665-2121

Appendix G (cont.)
Bureau of Land Management State Offices

Spokane District Office
1103 N. Fancher
Spokane, WA 99212-1275
509-536-1200
FAX: 509-536-1275

UTAH

Utah State Office
P.O. Box 45155
Salt Lake City, UT 84145-0155
801-539-4001
Fax: 801-539-4013
www.ut.blm.gov/

St. George Office
345 E. Riverside Dr.
St. George, UT 84720
435-688-3200
www.ut.blm.gov/st_george/index.html

Cedar City
176 East D.L. Sargent Dr.
Cedar City, UT 84720
435-586-2401
www.ut.blm.gov/cedar_city/
index.html

WYOMING and NEBRASKA

Wyoming State Office
5353 Yellowstone
P.O. Box 1828
Cheyenne,WY 82003
E-mail: _wymail@blm.gov
www.wy.blm.gov/

Newcastle
1101 Washington Blvd.
Newcastle, WY 82701-2972
307-746-4453
Fax: 307-746-4840
E-mail: newcastle_wymail@blm.gov
www.wy.blm.gov/directory/fo_map/
new_fo.html

Rawlins Office
1300 N. Third
P.O. Box 2407
Rawlins, WY 82301-2407
307-328-4200 or
307-328-4256
Fax: 307-328-4224
E-mail: rawlins_wymail@blm.gov
www.wy.blm.gov/directory/
fo_map/rawlins_fo.html

Glossary

Amortization- The term used to describe paying off a home loan in monthly installments. Home loans commonly amortize over 15, 20, 25, or 30 years.

Annual rate cap- The maximum interest rate increase or decrease permitted each year on an adjustable-rate mortgage.

Appraisal- A professionally prepared report that estimates the value of a property.

ARM (Adjustable Rate Mortgage)- A loan whose interest rate is adjusted periodically.

Assumability- The borrower's right to transfer a mortgage loan to a new buyer who meets the lender's credit standards.

Balloon mortgage- A mortgage that requires the entire outstanding balance to be paid in one lump sum on a certain date.

Buydown- Money given by a builder, relative, or other party which reduces the borrower's monthly mortgage payments in the first years of the mortgage.

Compound interest- Interest that is computed on both the principal and the accrued interest on a mortgage loan.

Curtailment- Partial prepayment of the principal on a mortgage.

Default- Failure to meet the payment terms of a mortgage contract.

Due-on-sale clause- A clause which allows the lender the right to demand payment in full if the property is sold.

ECOA (Equal Credit Opportunity Act)- A Federal law that forbids lenders and creditors from acts of discrimination when they extend credit.

Equity- Also referred to as owner's interest. Equity is the difference between the fair market value of a property and the amount owed on it.

Escrow payment- The portion of a monthly mortgage payment held by the lender to pay real estate taxes and insurance premiums.

Fair market value- The price a property would sell for in the current market between a willing buyer and a willing seller.

Fannie Mae- The common name of the Federal National Mortgage Association, a government-backed corporation which supplies lenders with money to fund mortgages.

FDIC (Federal Deposit Insurance Corporation)- A government-backed entity which insures deposits at banks and savings and loans, and also sells REO properties.

Federal Reserve System- America's central banking system, which is responsible for setting monetary policy and the discount rate, as well as influencing the availability of credit.

FHA (Federal Housing Administration)- An office within HUD which acts as an insurer of mortgages on residential properties.

Fixed mortgage- A mortgage which has a set interest rate for the entire term of the loan.

FmHA (Farmers Home Administration)- A former agency within the Department of Agriculture which is now known as RECDS (Rural Economic and Community Development Services).

Foreclosure- Legal proceedings in which a lender sells off a piece of real estate to recoup a borrower's unpaid debts on the property.

Freddie Mac (Federal Home Loan Mortgage Corporation)- A government-backed corporation that provides mortgage money to lenders nationwide.

GEM (Growing Equity Mortgage)- A mortgage in which annual increases in monthly payments reduce the outstanding principal and allow the loan to be paid off sooner.

GPM (Graduated Payment Mortgage)- A mortgage in which the monthly payments increase for a set period of time and then level off.

HECM (Home Equity Conversion Mortgage)- A loan which allows elderly homeowners to borrow against the equity they have in their homes and receive monthly payments.

HUD (U.S. Department of Housing and Urban Development)- An agency which offers affordable housing and special financing options for low to moderate income homebuyers.

Income limits- Legal limits on family income which must be met for admission to certain low and moderate income housing projects.

Income property- Real estate bought, owned, and/or operated with the intention of producing income.

Index- An independent measure of interest rates which is used to determine the rates for Adjustable Rate Mortgages and other mortgages where the interest paid changes over the entire life of the loan.

Interest rate cap- The limit on how much an interest rate can go up or down from year to year and over the entire life of the loan. This applies to an Adjustable Rate Mortgage.

Level-payment mortgage- A mortgage that offers a consistent, fixed monthly payment for the entire term of the loan.

Lien- A claim made by one person on the property of another person as a way of securing repayment of a debt.

Lock-out period- A set period of time during the term of a mortgage loan during which the loan cannot be prepaid, or paid off in advance.

LTV (Loan-To-Value Ratio)- The relationship between the appraised value of a property and the principal amount of the mortgage. Lenders use this ratio to tell borrowers the percentage of a property's value they are willing to finance.

Margin- Percentage points added to the Index to set new interest rates on an Adjustable Rate Mortgage at agreed-upon intervals.

Maturity- The date on which a loan obligation is due and payable in full.

MF (Multi-family)- Rental properties with four or more units.

Mortgage discount- See Points.

Mortgage insurance- Insurance that protects the lender in case the borrower defaults on a mortgage.

Mortgagee- The lender in a real estate transaction.

Mortgagor- The borrower in a real estate transaction.

Negative amortization- A loan repayment schedule in which the monthly payments are not large enough to cover the amount of interest due. The result is that the loan balance goes up instead of down.

Net worth- The value of all a borrower's assets, minus the amount of a borrower's total debts.

Origination fee- The fee charged by a lender to make a new mortgage. It usually includes a credit check and a property evaluation.

Payment cap- The maximum amount a monthly mortgage payment can go up or down at the end of each adjustment period (applies to Adjustable Rate Mortgages).

PITI (Principal, Interest, Taxes, and Insurance)- The four components of a traditional monthly mortgage payment.

PMI (Private Mortgage Insurance)- Insurance which protects the lender against default by the borrower.

Point- A one-time charge by a mortgage lender which occurs at closing. A point usually equals 1% of the principal on a mortgage loan.

Prepayment penalty- An extra charge to a borrower who pays their mortgage off early.

Principal- The amount of debt, aside from interest, that remains on a loan.

PUD (Planned Unit Development)- A housing development with one to four units located on land that also includes common property for the use of all the owners.

RECDS (Rural Economic and Community Development Services)- The new name for FmHA; and agency that sells rural and farm properties, and that offers both farm and nonfarm loans.

Refinancing- The act of replacing an old property loan with a now one, usually at a lower interest rate.

REO (Real Estate Owned)- A term that refers to ownership of property acquired as the result of foreclosure proceedings.

Truth in Lending Act- A law which requires creditors to make disclosures about the terms and cost of credit.

TLTV (Total Loan-To-Value Ratio)- The relationship between the appraised value of a piece of real estate and the principal amount of all mortgages on the property.

Underwriting- The review of a borrower's financial situation and the property for sale in order to determine the risk involved in making a real estate loan.

VA (Veterans Administration)- A Federal agency that sponsors many benefit programs for veterans, including guaranteed home loans. The VA also sells REO properties to both veterans and non-veterans.

Variable rate mortgage- A mortgage in which the interest rate may be adjusted up or down within agreed-upon limits.